CRAFT BOOK

Reproducible Craft Pages for Preschool and Elementary Students!

See our Special HomeLink Activities!

Noah's Park® Children's Church Craft Book (Blue Edition)

Product Developer:	Karen Pickering
Managing Editor:	Doug Schmidt
Editor:	Judy Gillispie
Contributing Writers:	Nancy Sutton
	Becca Koopmans
	Karen Schmidt
	René Stewart
	Darlene Franklin
	Gail Rohlfing
Craft Facilitator:	Judie Tippie
Interior Design:	Mike Riester; Dana Sherrer
Cover Design:	Todd Mock
Illustrations:	Aline Heiser
	Chris Sharp

Published by Cook Communications Ministries
4050 Lee Vance View · Colorado Springs, CO 80918-7100
www.cookministries.com

Printed in Canada.

ISBN: 0-7814-3864-0   101860

TABLE OF CONTENTS

Unit 5 *God Helped Jesus Grow and Learn*

Unit 6 *Jesus Did Good Things*

Unit 7 *God Gives Us His Special Son*

Unit 8 *God Gives Us a Wonderful World*

Unit 9 *God Gives Us What We Need to Live*

Unit 10 *God Loves Us*

Unit 11 *We Show Our Love to God*

Unit 12 *We Learn to Love One Another*

INTRODUCTION

The crafts included in this book coordinate with each lesson in the Noah's Park *Leader's Guide*. Each craft activity is designed to help reinforce the Bible story the children have heard and participated in during the lesson. The craft is also designed to help the children and their parents extend the learning even further by linking it to activities they can do at home during the following week.

If a craft is to be cut out and put together, be sure to include the HomeLink by gluing it to the back of the craft, enclosing it in a resealable plastic bag, or attaching it in some other way to be sent home.

You will notice the designation for the activities. **BCE** refers to the Elementary Craft in the Blue Edition of Noah's Park Children's Church. **BCP** refers to the Preschool Craft in the Blue Edition of the Noah's Park Children's Church. The number following that designation identifies the lesson number.

Each craft activity has a list of supplies listed which you will want to gather prior to your session. You may want to make one of the crafts in advance so that you can show the children what they will make. This will also assist the Park Patrol members as they help the children.

There are some basic supplies that you should keep on hand. These are listed below. Other supplies are more specialized and should be gathered as needed.

Pencils with erasers

Markers

Drawing Paper

Construction Paper (variety of colors, both 9" x 12" and 12" x 18")

Tape

Glue, paste, or glue sticks

Scissors

Craft Sticks

Paper fasteners, paper clips

Stapler and staples

Yarn, glitter, confetti

Resealable plastic bags (sandwich size)

BCE1: Bandage Holder

Supplies: Copies of the Bandage Holder and HomeLink · Self-adhesive bandages (one for each child) · Crayons or markers · Scissors · Tape or glue

Preparation: Make a copy of the Bandage Holder for each child on cardstock or white construction paper.

Directions: Give each child a copy of the Bandage Holder to color. Let the kids cut out their holder on the

solid lines. Help the kids fold their holder on the dotted lines and glue or tape the tabs. Give each child a self-adhesive bandage to put in it..

Read the title, I Care for My Family, and HomeLink to the children. Ask the kids where they could put their Bandage Holder at home as a reminder that God wants them to care for their families.

I Care for My Family

HomeLink: Exodus 1:6—2:10

God has given you a family that you can care for. How can you do this? Talk over some ideas with a parent. Ask permission to add more bandages to this holder. Whenever one is used, thank God for your family!

BCP1: Baby Moses in His Basket

Supplies: Copy of baby Moses and HomeLink for each child · "Clamshell"-shaped containers from a fast-food store (or cube-shaped facial tissue boxes, scissors, clear tape) · Yellow or brown poster paint · Liquid soap · Paintbrushes · Crayons · Paint shirts · Newspaper or table coverings

Preparation: Make copies of baby Moses and the HomeLink. Each child will need a small container that has a lid hinged on one side, such as are used in grocery store produce departments and fast food restaurants. (If you cannot find these, use cube-shaped tissue boxes: Tape paper over the hole; cut in half crosswise; tape the halves together on one side to form a hinge.) Mix a few drops of liquid soap into the paint to help it stick to the containers.

Directions: Wearing paintshirts and with the workspace covered, let each child paint the outside of a container (baby Moses' basket). As the containers dry, let each child color a baby Moses figure. Have the children put the figures in the baskets and glue the HomeLink to the inside of the top cover.

HomeLink: Exodus 1:6—2:10

God wants people in families to care for one another. God gave baby Moses a family that cared for him. Let your child use today's craft throughout the week to act out the Bible story:

The king of Egypt didn't want any of the Hebrews to have baby boys. A baby's mother loved her baby. She didn't want the king to hurt her baby. She hid the baby in a basket. Can you hide the baby? The princess found the baby in the basket. Can you open the basket?

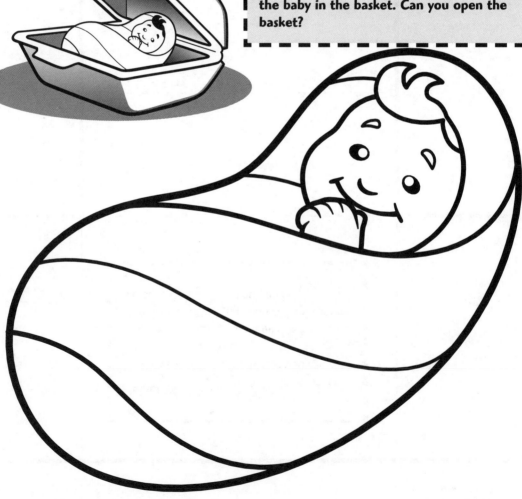

BCE2: Helping Hands Coupons

Supplies: Construction paper · Pencils · Scissors · Colored markers · Paper clips · Copies of the HomeLink

Directions: Have the kids trace their hands on construction paper and cut them out. Encourage them to make at least one handprint for each person in their family, plus one extra one to glue the HomeLink onto and keep as a reminder. As the kids work, explain how coupons work: They give the coupons to the people in their families; when the person needs what's on the coupon to be done, they give it back to the child and the child has to do it right then. Remind the kids that a good attitude is an important part of helping.

Brainstorm with the kids ideas of things they could do to help the people in their families this week. Write the ideas on the board in sentence form so the kids can copy them. (For example, "I'll do one of your chores for you," "I'll clean up my room," "I'll go fetch something you need," etc.) Encourage the kids to pick one idea for each person in their family and write it on one of their handprints. Let the Park Patrol help with writing as needed.

Let the kids decorate their Helping Hands Coupons with colored markers. When finished, have the kids paper clip their coupons together so they don't get

lost, along with their extra handprint with the HomeLink on it. Encourage the kids to give their coupons to their families after church.

I will make my bed without being asked.

I will feed the dog.

HomeLink: Exodus 3–5; 12
Moses's brother Aaron was a big help to him! God wants people in families to help one another. You can help the people in your family too! Here are things you can do:

Remember to give out the Helping Hand Coupons you made. And be sure to DO what you wrote when your family asks you to!

Remember to look for extra ways to help your family this week. Talk to your parents about ways you can be a helper.

Every day this week, say thank You to God for each person in your family.

BCP2: Moses Paper Bag Puppet

Supplies: Copies of the Moses puppet pieces and HomeLink · Lunch-size paper bags · Crayons · Glue · Optional: fabric scraps

Preparation: Make a copy of the Moses puppet pieces and HomeLink for each child. Cut out all the faces and clothes. If you are using the optional fabric, cut pieces for Moses' cloak.

Directions: Let the children color the puppet pieces. Show the children how to glue the puppet pieces to the bag. The HomeLink should be glued to the back of the puppet. Help the children make their puppets "talk" by moving the flap of the bag with their fingers. **In our Bible story God told Moses to talk to the king. Can you pretend that your Moses puppet is talking to the king?**

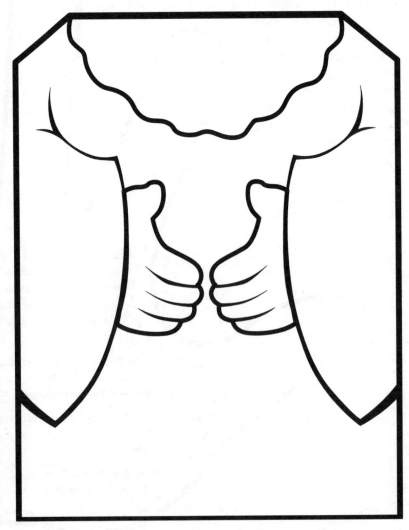

HomeLink: Exodus 3–5; 12

God wants people in families to help one another. Encourage your child to use the puppet throughout the week to act out the Bible story. Add stuffed animals and dolls to help create the scenes.

One day Moses was out watching his sheep. He saw a bush on fire that was not burning up. God talked to Moses out of the bush, "Go tell the king to let My people go. I will be with you. Your brother Aaron will help you."

Moses and Aaron went to the king. "Let God's people go," they said. The king said, "No!"

Many times Moses and Aaron talked to the king. Many times the king said, "No!" Finally the king told Moses and Aaron to take the people and leave Egypt.

BCE3: Help Me Learn Puppet

Supplies: Copies of the puppet and HomeLink · Scissors
· Pencils · Crayons · Markers · Glue · Lunch-size paper bags
· Optional: fabric scraps

Preparation: Make a copy of the puppet pieces and
HomeLink for each child. If you are using the optional
fabric, cut out pieces to use for clothing.

Directions: Give each child a copy of the puppet
pieces. Read the HomeLink aloud with the entire
class. Talk about the ways the kids could learn from a
family member this week. Ask the kids to color the
puppet to resemble a family member they would choose
to learn from this week.

When the puppets are colored, pass out the paper bags and
scissors. Then ask the kids to cut out their puppets and glue
them onto the paper bags. The HomeLink should be glued to
the back of the puppet. If you are using the optional fabric
scraps, encourage the kids to cut out clothing that would
make their puppet look like the family member they
have chosen to learn from.

When the puppets are complete, give the kids a
chance to practice "talking" with their
puppets.

HomeLink: Exodus 18

Moses learned from his wife's father,
Jethro. You can learn from your family
too. What could you learn from each
person in your family?

This week look for a way to learn from
your family every day. Every night at
bedtime, tell a parent what you
learned. Pray together to thank God
for that family member.

BCP3: Helper Buttons

Supplies: Copies of the buttons and HomeLink
· Washable markers · Scissors · Resealable plastic bags

Preparation: Copy a set of buttons and a HomeLink for each child.

Directions: Let each child color a set of helper buttons.

We can help in our families just as Jethro helped Moses. What are some ways you help in your family? Let the children talk about ways they can be helpers at home. **Each time you are a helper at home this week, leave a helper button in that spot when you are done.**

Let children cut out their buttons. You may need to help younger children cut theirs. Put each child's buttons and a HomeLink in a resealable plastic bag. Write each child's name on his or her bag.

HomeLink: Exodus 18

Your child is being encouraged to be a helper at home this week! Each time your child helps, he or she may leave in that spot one of the Helper Buttons made in class. You may "help" your child by reminding him or her to use the buttons.

Read the Bible story with your child during the week: **Who was traveling a long, long way?** Pat your knees as if walking. **Moses and the Hebrews. Who came to see Moses?** Put your hand above your eyes as if looking. **Jethro, the father of Moses' wife. Who else came to see Moses?** Put your hand above your eyes. **People who had problems. Moses helped them all day long. What did Jethro tell Moses?** Cup your hands around your mouth. **"You can't help them all by yourself. You need some help!" What did Moses do?** Point to your child. **He asked good people to help him.**

BCE4: Family Crest

Supplies: Copies of the crest and HomeLink · Scissors · Colored pencils · Optional: additional craft supplies, such as construction paper, glitter glue, etc.

Preparation: Make a copy of the crest and a HomeLink for each child. Make a sample crest about your own family.

Directions: Show the children your sample family crest and explain why you put on the things you did. Ask the kids to think about things they love about being in their family. Help them think of ways to draw pictures or symbols that represent those things.

Encourage creativity. For example, a family that sticks close together might be represented by a jar of peanut butter. A family that never misses their kids' sporting events might be represented by a pair of binoculars. If a child loves bedtime stories or family reading times, a book might represent that.

Then give each child a crest to draw on, decorate, and cut out. Encourage the kids to draw a picture in each section and their family name across the top. The HomeLink may be glued to the back.

HomeLink: Ruth 1—4

Ruth showed love to her mother-in-law, Naomi. God wants us to love our families. What do you love about your family? Draw some of those things on your Family Crest. Show your Family Crest to your family this week.

BCP4: Ruth Bible Story Puppets

Supplies: A set of puppets and a HomeLink for each child · Five craft sticks for each child · Crayons · Tape · Resealable plastic bags

Preparation: Copy a set of puppets and a HomeLink for each child, and cut them out.

Directions: Help the children identify the five puppets. Let each child color a set of five puppets. Help the children tape the top half of a craft stick to the back of each puppet. Each child can take a set of puppets and a HomeLink home in a resealable plastic bag.

HomeLink: Ruth 1–4

Help your child act out the Bible story with the stick puppets. **Ruth lived with Naomi. Ruth went to a field where workers were cutting grain. Ruth picked up the leftover grain. Ruth took the grain home to Naomi so they could make bread. Boaz told the workers to give Ruth more grain. Boaz and Ruth got married. They had a baby named Obed. Ruth showed her love to Naomi. God wants us to love our families.**

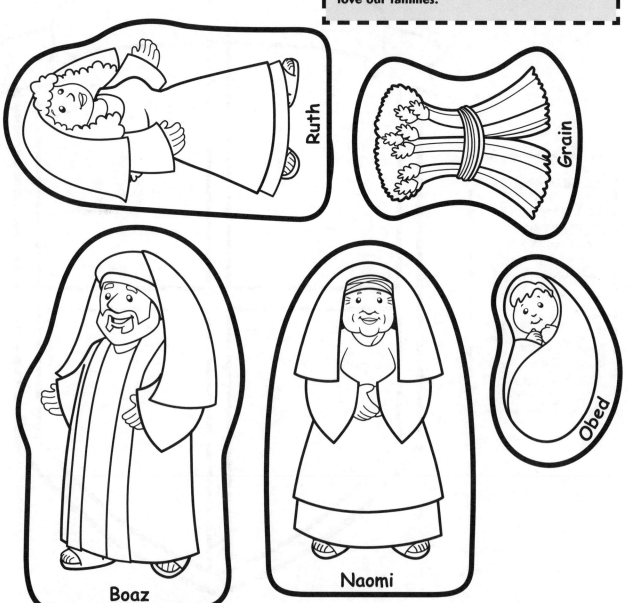

Ruth

Grain

Boaz

Naomi

Obed

BCE5: Prayer Cube

Supplies: Copies of the cube outline · Cardstock or heavy paper · Scissors · Glue · Prayer Spinners made during Share and Prayer

Preparation: On cardstock or heavy paper, make a copy of the cube outline for each child.

Directions: Have the kids cut out the cubes on the solid lines, fold on the dotted lines, and glue the tabs to form Prayer Cubes. Distribute the kids' Prayer Spinners made during Share and Prayer time. The children use their spinners and cubes to do a prayer activity:

A child spins the spinner to find out which friend to pray for. Then the child tosses the Prayer Cube to find out what to pray. For example, if the spinner points to "Chris" and the cube lands with the phrase "to love Jesus" facing up, then the child could pray

that Jesus would help Chris learn to love Him more.

The kids may do the activity individually or in small groups. Put the HomeLink, cube, and spinner in a resealable bag to send home with each child.

HomeLink: John 12:1-3

God gives us friends! Even Jesus had friends. Use your Prayer Spinner and Prayer Cube together to help you pray for your friends. Ask a parent to play with you. Here's how it works:

Spin your spinner. You'll pray for the friend it lands on. Toss your cube. You'll pray about whatever lands facing up.

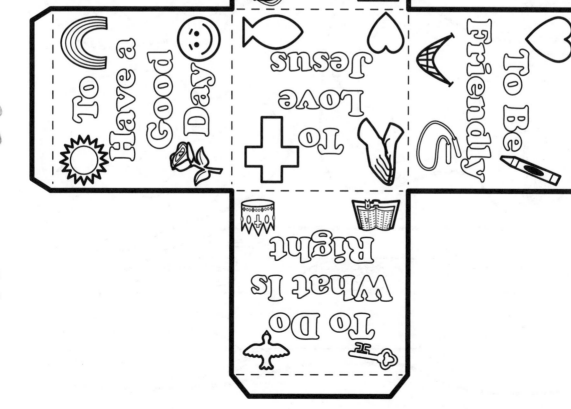

BCP5: Jesus' Friends Flannel Figures

Supplies: One set of figures and a HomeLink for each child · Colored pencils · Felt · Glue · Resealable plastic bags

Preparation: Copy a set of the five figures and a HomeLink for each child. Cut them out. Cut five 1-inch squares of felt for each child.

Directions: Give each child a set of five figures to color. Talk about who they are. Help the children glue a felt square to the back of each figure. Place each child's figures and a HomeLink in a resealable plastic bag with their name on it.

HomeLink: John 12:1-3

Three of Jesus' special friends were sisters and brother—Mary, Martha, and Lazarus. Let your child use the flannel figures on an upholstered chair or a fuzzy blanket that the felt will stick to. Play the following "Show Me" game to review the Bible story during the week.

Show me Jesus' friend and Jesus sitting at a table (Lazarus). **Show me Jesus' friend who served Him food** (Martha). **Show me Jesus' friend who gave Him a special gift of perfume** (Mary). **Show me all of Jesus' friends** (Lazarus, Martha, Mary).

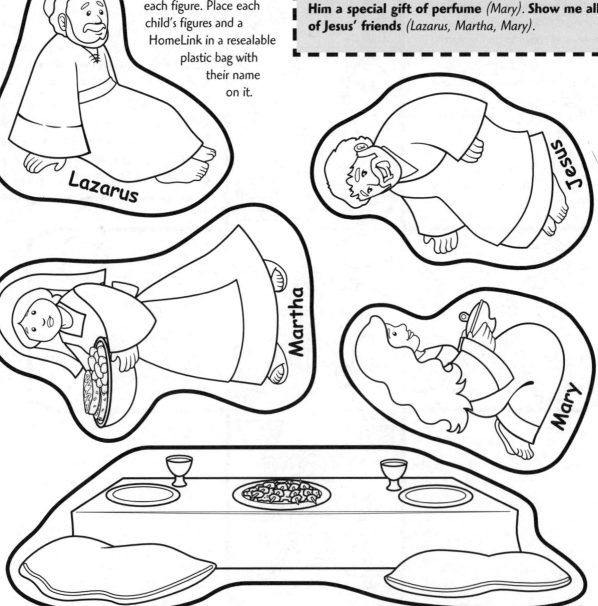

BCE6: Special Friend Badge

Supplies: Copies of the badge and HomeLink · Cardstock or heavy paper · Colored markers · Hole punch · Ribbon or yarn · Scissors · Optional: additional art supplies, such as glitter glue, sequins, etc.

Preparation: Make a copy of the badge on cardstock or heavy paper for each child. Make copies of the HomeLink on regular paper.

Directions: Give each child a copy of the "Jesus Is My Special Friend" badge. Let the kids color and decorate the front of the badge. Give each child a HomeLink paragraph to glue on the back of the badge.

When finished, punch a hole near the top and put ribbon or yarn through it so the kids can wear the badge around their neck. Remind the children that the badge can also remind them to talk to their special friend, Jesus.

HomeLink: Mark 10:13-16

Jesus wants to be your special friend. He loves kids! You can talk to Jesus anytime, about anything. Take time to talk to Him every day this week.

BCP6: Jesus and the Children Picture

Supplies: Copies of the coloring picture and HomeLink · Crayons · Fabric scraps · Glue · Construction paper

Preparation: Copy a picture and HomeLink for each child. Cut the fabric scraps into pieces no larger than 1" square.

Directions: Give each child a "Jesus and the Children" picture to color. When done, let the children glue fabric pieces on the people's clothes for texture. Mount each picture on construction paper. Glue a HomeLink to the back of each picture.

HomeLink: Mark 10:13-16

God gives your child friends—and friendship with Jesus is extra special. Put this picture in a place where your child can be reminded of this friendship. Review the Bible story during the week.

Mommies and daddies brought their children to see Jesus so He could bless them. Jesus' helpers sent the families away. Maybe they thought Jesus was too busy to spend time with children. But Jesus told His helpers to let the families come back. Jesus loved the children. Jesus held the children. Jesus is our special friend.

BCE7: Friendship Frame

Supplies: Several colors of poster board · Scissors · Magnetic tape · Ruler · Pencil · Small craft foam shapes · Glue · Glitter glue

Preparation: Cut poster board into 6" x 8" rectangles, two for each child. From half of the rectangles, cut out the center to leave an opening 3" x 5" (to hold a 4" x 6" photo). Cut magnetic tape into one-inch pieces, two for each child **or** cut a triangular cardboard shape to use as a stand.

Directions: Give each child a cut-out poster board frame to decorate. The kids may glue on craft foam shapes or use glitter glue.

When done, give each child a solid poster board rectangle to use as a frame back. Instruct the children to glue it only to the bottom and two sides of their frame, and to put glue only along the outer edges. This will allow a photo to be slipped in the top and tucked in behind the front of the frame. Glue the HomeLink to the back along with two magnet pieces or the triangular stand.

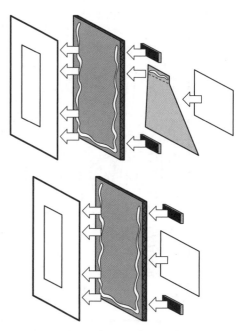

HomeLink: Mark 2:1-12

The man who couldn't walk had four friends who helped him get to Jesus. God gives you friends too. You and your friends can help each other.

Think about your friends. Find a picture of one friend (or a group!) to put in your frame. Let this picture remind you to thank God for your friends.

BCP7: Picture Book

Supplies: Copy of the pictures and HomeLink · Crayons · Stapler

Preparation: Copy and cut out the story panels and HomeLink for each child.

Directions: Give each child a set of story panels to color. Talk about the Bible story while they are coloring. Help each child assemble a book in order by page numbers. The title page should be the first page and the HomeLink should be the last page.

2

3

4

HomeLink: Mark 2:1-12

Let your child "read" this book to you throughout the week.

Page 1: Four friends carry the man on the mat to see Jesus.

Page 2: It is so crowded that they take him up on the roof.

Page 3: The friends dig a hole in the roof and lower their friend down to Jesus.

Page 4: Jesus heals the man so that he can walk.

6

5

1

4 FRIENDS ARE HELPERS

BCE8: Faith Flag

Supplies: Copies of the HomeLink and "stickers" below · Construction paper or felt · Scissors · Glue · Colored markers · Optional: additional craft supplies, such as glitter glue or other decorative material

Preparation: Make copies of the "stickers" and HomeLink for each child. Cut large pennant shapes from construction paper or felt.

Directions: Remind the children that in today's Bible story, the centurion had faith in Jesus to help his friends. Your class will make flags to remind them to ask Jesus to help their friends as well.

Let each child choose a pennant to decorate. Let the kids choose from among the "stickers" to glue on their flags or draw their own symbols to represent praying for friends. Have the kids each glue a HomeLink to the back.

Use whatever time and supplies you have left to let the children further decorate their Faith Flags.

HomeLink: Luke 7:1-10

The Roman centurion learned that Jesus could help his servant friend. Jesus can help your friends too. Show your Faith Flag to your parents, and talk about why you picked the pictures you did. Ask your parents to pray for your friends with you.

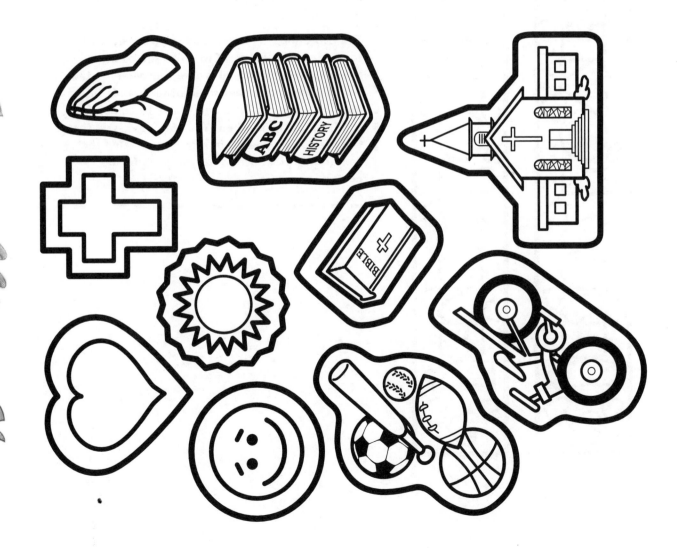

BCP8: Friendship Bracelets

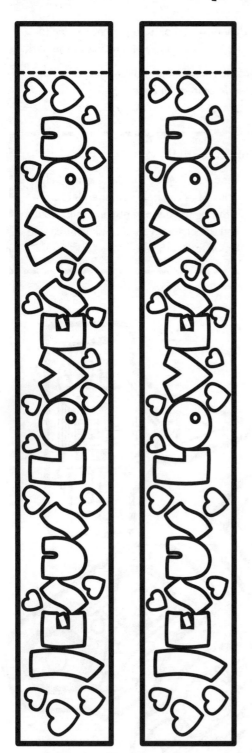

Supplies: Copies of the bracelets and HomeLink · Crayons · Tape · Resealable plastic bags

Preparation: Copy two bracelets and a HomeLink for each child. Cut them out.

Directions: Give each child two bracelets to color. Help the children tape each bracelet so that the tab is attached to the other end. Encourage the children to wear one bracelet and give the other to a friend. Send the friend's bracelet and the HomeLink home in a resealable plastic bag.

HomeLink: Luke 7:1-10

Encourage your child to give one of the friendship bracelets to a friend. Here's a review story to read together during the week.

The centurion's servant friend was very sick. The town leaders asked Jesus to go to the centurion's house to help the friend. While they were on their way, the centurion sent some other friends with a message for Jesus: "You don't have to come. You can help him from where You are." Jesus said that the centurion believed in Him. Jesus healed the centurion's friend without ever going to the centurion's house.

BCE9: Share Dough

Supplies: Children's modeling clay or homemade clay using the recipe provided · Copies of the HomeLink · Waxed paper · Cardboard squares · Pencil

Preparation: If you wish to make your own clay, prepare the recipe provided.

Directions: Give each child a piece of waxed paper to use as a work mat and a handful of clay. Let the children handle and knead it as you talk together about symbols that remind them of sharing and friendship. They might suggest a fish, a cross, a child, a heart, and so on. Encourage each child to choose a symbol to mold with their clay.

When finished, let each child place his or her clay artwork on a cardboard square to dry and take home. Use pencil to write kids' names on their cardboard. Place a HomeLink with each child's artwork to take home.

Play Dough Recipe

2 c. flour

1 c. salt

4 T. cream of tartar

1 pkg. unsweetened dry drink mix for scent and color

2 c. warm water

2 T. cooking oil

Stir over medium heat until mixture pulls away from sides to form a ball. Store in airtight container. (For eight to ten children.)

HomeLink: John 6:5-13

A boy shared his little lunch with Jesus, and Jesus used it to feed over 5,000 people! Jesus can help you share too. Talk with your parents about how your clay artwork can be a reminder to you of sharing.

BCP9: Basket of Fish and Bread

Supplies: Copies of the fish, bread, and HomeLink · Plastic berry or produce baskets · Crayons · Scissors · Chenille wire

Preparation: Ask a produce department for donations of plastic berry baskets for your class. Make copies of the fish, loaves, and HomeLink for each child. Cut out the HomeLinks.

Directions: Give each child a page with fish and bread on it. Let the children color their fish and bread and cut them out. Show the children how to make a handle on their baskets by bending a chenille wire into a loop, and then twisting each end of the loop onto the basket. Put the fish, bread, and a HomeLink in each basket to take home.

HomeLink: John 6:5-13

A boy shared his lunch with Jesus, and He used it to feed 5,000 people! Encourage your child to use the basket to act out the Bible story at home.

Many people listened to Jesus one day, but they got hungry. A little boy had a lunch of fish and bread. He shared his lunch with Jesus. Jesus made the lunch big enough to feed all of the people.

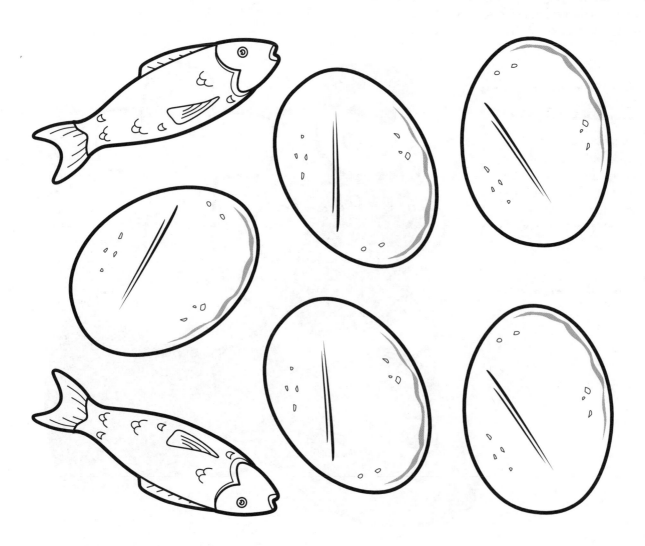

BCE10: Pop-up Poster

Supplies: Copies of the Bible story picture and HomeLink · Colorful construction paper · Ruler · Scissors · Colored markers · Glue or tape

Preparation: Copy the picture and HomeLink for each child. Cut construction paper into 7" wide x 6" high rectangles.

Directions: Give each child a Bible story picture to color and cut out on the solid line. Have the kids each fold their picture on the fold lines as shown in the diagram.

Pass out the construction paper rectangles and have the kids fold it in half, so it has a book shape. On the front cover, the kids write "BIBLE." On the back cover, they glue a HomeLink. Then have the kids tape the edges of their folded pictures into the book shape so that the picture folds when they close the cover. It will "pop up" when they open the book. On the inside top part of their books, ask the kids to write the story title: "God's people learn from the Bible."

HomeLink: Luke 4:16-22

God's people learn from the Bible. Jesus taught from God's Word. How can you learn from the Bible? Talk over some ideas with your parents.

BCP10: Bible Storybook

Supplies: Copies of the book covers · Scissors · Blank paper · Crayons · Stapler · Glue sticks

Preparation: Copy both book covers for each child. Cut them out. Cut blank paper into 4" x 5" rectangles.

Directions: Give each child three or four paper rectangles to serve as pages. Have each child color a picture of a favorite Bible story on each page. For example, they might color a rainbow for the Noah's Ark story, plants and animals for the Creation story, Jesus welcoming children for that story, or two coins for today's story. The Park Patrol should write the names of the stories on the pages for the children.

Put each book together by stapling the pages inside a set of covers. Be sure the children add their names to their Bible Storybooks.

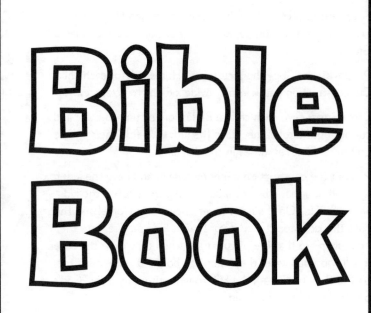

HomeLink: Luke 4:16–22

God gives us the Church, and God's people learn from the Bible. Help your child act out a Bible-time worship service at a synagogue. The Bible Storybook can be the "scroll." This story review may help.

Everyone went to the synagogue to worship God. They prayed. They sang. Then Jesus stood up and read God's Word. After He was done, Jesus rolled up the scroll and sat down. Jesus helped the people understand God's Word. He said that God had sent Him to do what the Bible verses said.

BCE11: Coin Cups

Supplies: Copies of the HomeLink · Paper or foam cups · Felt or fabric · Rubber bands (a size that will fit the top circumference of the cup) · Ribbon · Scissors · Glitter glue

Preparation: Measure the circumference of the top of the paper cup, and cut felt or fabric circles about two inches wider than that. In the center of each fabric piece, cut a coin-size slit with sharp scissors. Also cut ribbon eight inches longer than the circumference. Have a cup, a felt/fabric circle, a ribbon, a rubber band, and a copy of the HomeLink for each child.

Directions: Show the children how to place a felt or fabric circle over the top of the cup and hold it in place with a rubber band. Have the children tie a ribbon around the rubber band to cover it. Glue the HomeLink to the outside of the cup. Then let the children use glitter glue to decorate or draw a border around the bottom portion of their cup.

Read together the HomeLink, and encourage the children to keep offerings in their Coin Cup. Allow time for the glitter glue to dry.

HomeLink: Mark 12:41-44

God's people give their offerings. The poor woman in the Bible story teaches us that even though she gave just a little, she really gave a lot!

Talk to your parents about how you can give some of your money as an offering to God. You might only have a little to give, but if you give from your heart, it's really a lot! You can keep the money in your Coin Cup.

BCP11: Movable Poster

Supplies: Copies of the poster pieces and HomeLink · Scissors · Crayons · Glue sticks · Brass paper fasteners · Paper clips

Preparation: Copy the poster, arm, coins, and HomeLink for each child, and cut them out. Use a sharp point to open the slit in the offering container on each page.

Directions: Give each child a picture, the woman's arm, and two coins to color. While the children color, talk about what the woman did in the Bible story. Help each child put a brass paper fastener through the "x" on the movable arm, then through the "x" on the woman's shoulder in the picture. Let each child glue a HomeLink to the back of the picture, avoiding the slit. Show the children how to move the woman's arm so that she puts the coins into the offering container. Use a paper clip to attach the coins to each child's picture to send home.

HomeLink: Mark 12:41-44

God's people give their offerings. Let your child use this picture to tell you the Bible story.

One day Jesus was in the temple. Rich people brought money to put in the offering container. They gave a little from all they had. A poor woman came and gave two pennies. That was everything she had. Jesus said that the poor woman gave the most to God.

BCE12: Prayer Pinwheel

Supplies: Copies of the pinwheel · Colored paper · Straws · Brass-plated paper fasteners · Glue sticks · Scissors

Preparations: Copy the pinwheel on colorful paper, one for each child, and cut them out.

Directions: Give each child a copy of the pinwheel with the HomeLink. Read all the words to the class. Then show the kids how to fold the pinwheel square in half on the dotted lines to make a triangle. Then fold in half again. Unfold the pinwheel squares. On each fold, the children cut halfway down, to the hash-marks.

The children bend the point of each triangle with no writing toward the center circle and secure with a dab of glue. Then push a paper fastener through the center (all layers) and in through the top of a straw. You may need to help by poking a small hole with a pair of sharp scissors.

Encourage the kids to use their Prayer Pinwheels during the week to help them pray.

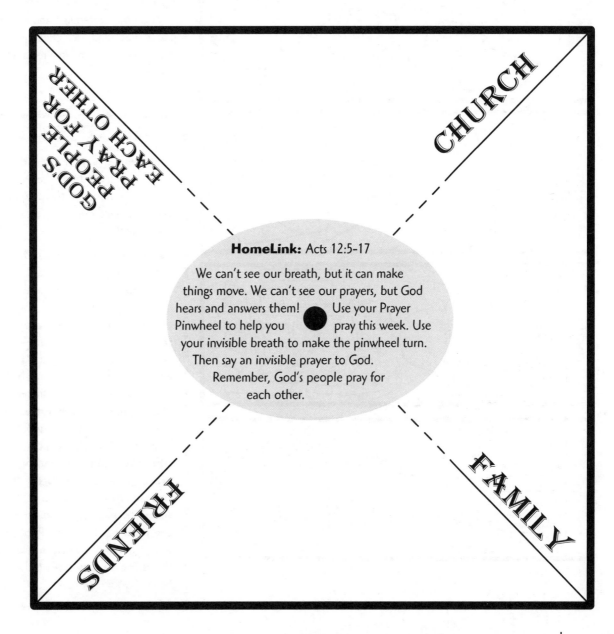

GOD'S PEOPLE PRAY FOR EACH OTHER

CHURCH

HomeLink: Acts 12:5-17

We can't see our breath, but it can make things move. We can't see our prayers, but God hears and answers them! Use your Prayer Pinwheel to help you pray this week. Use your invisible breath to make the pinwheel turn. Then say an invisible prayer to God. Remember, God's people pray for each other.

FRIENDS

FAMILY

BCP12: Peter Finger Puppets

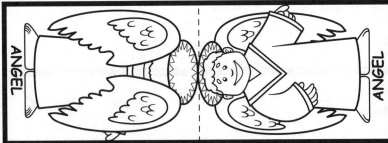

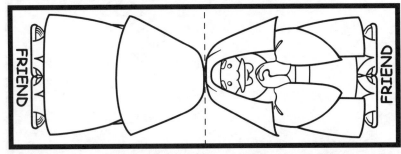

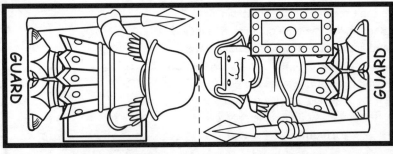

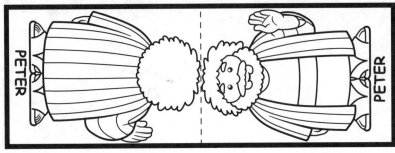

Supplies: Copies of the puppets and HomeLink for each child · Crayons or markers · Clear tape · Resealable plastic bags

Preparation: Copy a set of five puppets and a HomeLink for each child. Cut them apart.

Directions: Give each child a set of five puppets to color. Show the children how to color both halves of each puppet the same. Help the children fold each puppet on the dotted line and tape the top and sides. Send each child's puppets and a HomeLink home in a resealable plastic bag.

HomeLink: Acts 12:5-17

God's people pray for each other. The church prayed for Peter when he was in prison. Use the puppets with your child during the week to retell the story.

Peter was in jail because he told about Jesus. Soldiers guarded him. Put Peter and the guard puppets on your left hand. **Peter's church friends prayed for him.** Put the praying friend puppet on your right hand. **An angel came to the jail.** Add the angel puppet to your left hand. **The angel led Peter out of the jail.** Take off the guard puppet. **Peter went to the house where his church friends were praying.** Take off the angel. **The servant, Rhoda, was so surprised she forgot to open the door for him!** Add Rhoda to your right hand. **But then she let Peter in. He was safe!** Move Peter to your right hand.

BCE13: Care Clips

Supplies: Copies of the church picture and HomeLink
· Spring-type clothespins · Narrow magnetic tape
· Colored pencils · Scissors · Glue · Optional: pictures of
your church or church leaders

Preparation: Copy the church picture and HomeLink
for each child. Cut the magnetic tape into 3" strips.

Directions: Give each child a church picture to color.
As the children work, talk about who are leaders in
your church, from pastoral staff to Sunday school
teachers. (Option: Give each child a picture of your
church rather than coloring the drawing below.)

When finished, have the kids glue their picture to one
side of a clothespin. Show them how to remove the
backing from a piece of magnetic tape and attach it to
the other side of the clothespin. Give each child a
HomeLink to put in the Care Clip. If you have pictures
of church leaders, give each child one to also put in the
clip.

Encourage the kids to pray for the leaders of your church
this week. The kids may hang their Care Clips on a
refrigerator or any other metal surface.

HomeLink: Acts 20:16-38

God gives us the Church. And He gives church
leaders to care for His people.

Talk with your parents about who are the leaders in
your church. What can you pray for them? Pray
together with your parents. Thank God for giving us
the Church.

BCP13: Paul Trading Cards

Supplies: Copies of the Trading Cards and HomeLink · Colored pencils · Glue sticks · Resealable plastic bags

Preparation: On stiff paper, copy a set of Trading Cards and a HomeLink for each child. Cut them apart.

Directions: Give each child a set of trading cards to color. Help the children fold the cards on the dotted line. Show them how to glue the fronts and backs together to create the cards. Send the trading cards and a HomeLink home in a resealable plastic bag.

HomeLink: Acts 20:16-38

God gives us the Church. It is made up of God's people. Church leaders care for God's people. Help your child use the Trading Cards during the week to review the Bible story of Paul and the church leaders from Ephesus.

Paul

I tell people about Jesus.

I prayed with the church leaders from Ephesus before I went to Jerusalem.

Paul

Leaders from Ephesus

We are leaders of the church.

We prayed with Paul before he went to Jerusalem.

Leaders from Ephesus

Boat

I take people from place to place.

I took Paul to Jerusalem so he could tell more people about Jesus.

Boat

BCE14: Message Megaphones

Supplies: Copies of the megaphones and "stickers" · Crayons or colored pencils · Scissors · Glue · Tape

Preparation: Make a copy of the megaphone and "stickers" for each child.

Directions: Give each child a copy of the megaphone page and "stickers." Give the children time to color the "stickers." Then have the children cut out and glue the "stickers" onto the megaphone. Be sure the children understand which portion of the megaphone will be covered up when rolled so they don't glue stickers there. Then the children cut out their megaphones along the solid lines, curve it into a cone shape, and tape together. When finished, children can use their Message Megaphones to announce Jesus' coming and to say the memory verse.

START ROLLING HERE

TAPE HERE

HomeLink: Read the Bible story with your parents: Luke 1:26-38; Matthew 1:18-25.

Use your megaphone this week to announce to your family that Jesus is coming. It can also help you practice saying your Bible memory verse.

BCP14: Nativity Figures, Part One

Supplies: Copies of the Mary, Joseph, and angel figures and a HomeLink for each child · Three 2" x 4" pieces of wood or three cardboard tubes for each child · Crayons · Glue · Gallon-size resealable plastic bags

Preparation: Cut out the figures and HomeLinks. Cut the 2" x 4" wood or the cardboard tubes into 3" lengths. Lightly sand the ends of the wood.

Directions: Give each child a figure of Mary, Joseph, and an angel to color. Help the children glue each figure to either a piece of wood or a cardboard tube so that they stand up. Send home the figures and a copy of the HomeLink in a resealable bag.

HomeLink: Luke 1:26-38; Matthew 1:18-25

Over the next three weeks your child will make a nativity set and learn how God sent His Son, Jesus. Encourage your child to play with the figures throughout the week. The following questions can help your child's play.

Who came to visit Mary? *(The angel.)* **What was the angel's message?** *(You will have a baby, God's Son.)* **Who else saw an angel?** *(Joseph.)* **What did the angel tell Joseph?** *(Mary will have a baby, God's Son.)*

BCE15: Birth Certificate for Baby Jesus

Supplies: Copies of the birth certificate and HomeLink (one for each child) · Colored pencils

Directions: Give each child a copy of the Birth Certificate for Baby Jesus. Work together with the children to help them fill out the missing information. Then allow the children to color and decorate their certificates. Correct answers: *Child's name: Jesus; Date of birth: around 4 B.C.; Place of birth: Bethlehem; Mother's*

name: Mary; Father's name: God; Earthly father's name: Joseph; Earthly father's Job: carpenter. Glue the HomeLink to the back.

> **HomeLink:** Luke 2:1-7
> Celebrate Jesus' birth by showing this paper to at least three people in your family.

BIRTH CERTIFICATE

This paper states the true record of this child's birth.

Recorded by the

Leaders in Bethlehem in Judea.

Child's Name: _____

Date of Birth: _____

Place of Birth: _____

Mother's Name: _____

Father's Name: _____

Earthly

Father's Name: _____

Earthly Father's Job Title: _____

BCP15: Nativity Figures, Part Two

Supplies: Copy of the donkey and baby Jesus figures and a HomeLink for each child · Two 2" x 4" pieces of wood or two cardboard tubes for each child · Crayons · Glue · Gallon-size resealable plastic bags

Preparation: Cut out the figures and HomeLinks. Cut the 2" x 4" wood or the cardboard tubes into 3" lengths. Lightly sand the ends of the wood.

Directions: Give each child a figure of a donkey and baby Jesus to color. Help the children glue each figure to either a piece of wood or a cardboard tube so that they stand up. Send home the figures and a copy of the HomeLink in a resealable bag.

HomeLink: Luke 2:1-7

This week your child made the nativity figures of baby Jesus and a donkey. These go along with last week's figures of Mary, Joseph, and an angel. As your child plays with the figures during the week, emphasize the happy news: "Jesus is born!" Use this story summary to help your child play with the nativity figures:

Mary and Joseph went to Bethlehem. The only place they could find to stay was in a stable, where animals were kept. There baby Jesus was born.

BCE16: Angel and Shepherd Cutouts

Supplies: Copies of angel and shepherd figures · Cardstock or heavy paper · Scissors · Crayons or colored pencils · Resealable plastic bags

Preparation: On card stock or heavy paper, make TWO copies of the angel and shepherd figures for each child. Also make a copy of the HomeLink for each child.

Directions: Have each child cut out four figures—two angels and two shepherds. On one of each set of identical shapes, cut from the top down to the dot; on the other cut from the bottom up to the dot. Children can color figures to portray angels and shepherds. Make the figures 3-dimensional by slotting together the two pieces at the slit. Have Park Patrol staff on hand to guide the cutting and assembling process. When finished, each child's pair of figures should stand up on their own. Give each child a HomeLink to take home with the figures. Place the figures and the HomeLink in a resealable plastic bag to take home.

HomeLink: Luke 2:8-18

There's good news for everyone! The angels brought the good news of Jesus' birth to the shepherds. Read the Bible story with your parents. Then use your angel and shepherd to act out the story for them.

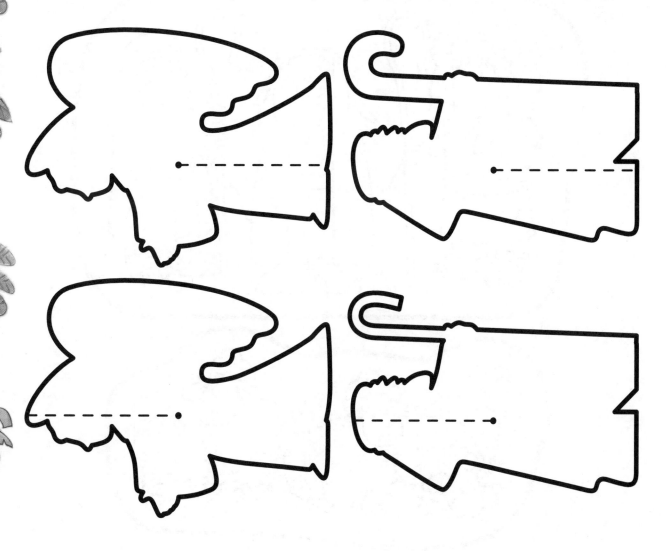

BCP16: Nativity Figures, Part Three

Supplies: Copies of the shepherds and sheep figures and a HomeLink for each child · Two 2" x 4" pieces of wood or two cardboard tubes for each child · Crayons · Glue · Gallon-size resealable plastic bags

Preparation: Cut out the figures and HomeLinks. Cut the 2" x 4" wood or the cardboard tubes into 3" lengths. Lightly sand the ends of the wood.

Directions: Give each child a figure of the shepherds and the sheep to color. Help the children glue each figure to either a piece of wood or a cardboard tube. Send home the figures and a copy of the HomeLink in a resealable bag.

HomeLink: Luke 2:8-18

In today's Bible story, your child heard the angel tell the shepherds that Jesus, God's Son, was born! Encourage your child to act out this story using the nativity figures made over the past weeks:

The angel told the shepherds, "Jesus is born!" The shepherds looked for baby Jesus. The shepherds found Mary and Joseph. They found baby Jesus. The shepherds told other people, "Jesus is God's Son!"

BCE17: Simeon and Anna Reminder

Supplies: Paper plates · Construction paper · Felt · Scissors · Glue · Cotton balls or white or gray yarn · Markers

Preparation: Using the templates, cut felt circles from any flesh-tone felt. Cut felt triangles from any color of felt. The circle will be Jesus' head, the triangle will be His blanket. Have one head and one blanket for each child. Make a copy of the HomeLink for each child.

Directions: Let each child choose whether to make Simeon or Anna, and give each child a paper plate to use as the head. The children draw facial features on the plate and glue cotton balls or white or gray yarn along the top and side edge to make hair. Then the children use construction paper to cut out a simple robe. Glue the top of the robe to the bottom of the face. Each child should also glue a HomeLink to the back of the paper plate head.

When Anna or Simeon is completed, the children may draw a face on a felt circle and glue it to a felt blanket to make baby Jesus swaddled in a blanket. Then they glue baby Jesus to the body of Anna or Simeon, as if they are holding Him.

HomeLink: Luke 2:21-38

Simeon and Anna were both older people who loved God very much. God let them know that Jesus was His Son. Anna and Simeon were very excited to see Jesus!

Anna's and Simeon's stories are part of the proof that Jesus is God's Son. Who can you tell this week that Jesus is God's Son?

BCP17: Shiny Doorknob Hanger

Supplies: Cardstock or heavy paper · Paint shirts · Glue · Washable watercolor paints · Paintbrushes · Salt in a shaker · Small containers of water

Preparation: Make copies of the doorknob hanger on cardstock, one for each child. Copy the HomeLink on regular paper.

Directions: Have each child wear a paint shirt. First the children each glue a HomeLink to the back of a doorknob hanger. Then let the children paint the front of the doorknob hanger. While the paint is still wet, help each child sprinkle salt on the paint. When the paint dries, the salt crystals will glitter.

HomeLink: Luke 2:21-38

Simeon and Anna, two elderly people who loved God, recognized that baby Jesus was God's Son. Let your child choose a place to put this Shiny Doorknob Hanger as a reminder of this truth.

Take time this week to act out the Bible story with your child. One of you pretends to be both Mary and Joseph. The other plays the parts of Simeon and Anna. **Mary and Joseph took Jesus to the temple. They saw Simeon there. Simeon prayed, "Thank You, God, for sending us Your Son, Jesus." Then they saw Anna. Anna prayed, "Thank You, God, for sending Your Son, Jesus."**

BCE18: Maze of Caring

Supplies: Copies of the maze and HomeLink · Colored pencils · Glue

Preparation: Make a copy of the maze and HomeLink for each child.

Directions: Give each child a copy of the maze and HomeLink. Have them start by writing their name on it. Next, have the kids glue the HomeLink to the back of the maze. Read the directions together. Then let the children work individually on the maze.

HomeLink: Matthew 2:13-15, 19-23

God used Mary and Joseph to take care of Jesus when He was a child on earth. Talk with your parents about all the different people that God uses to take care of you. Let this maze take you through your week! Every time you come to someone who cares for you, stop and color the picture. Take time to pray and thank God for each of them.

BCP18: Picture-Words Banner

Supplies: Copy of the hieroglyphics (picture-words) and a HomeLink for each child · Scissors · Crayons · Felt · Glue

Preparation: Cut felt into strips 3" x 12".

Directions: Give each child a copy of the five hieroglyphic squares, and explain that when Jesus lived in Egypt, people used pictures to stand for letters or words. Help the children find the five letters in the name "Jesus"—one in each square. The numbers 1 through 5 will be a clue for the children. Then let the children color the pictures and then cut out the squares. Help the children glue them in order on a felt strip. Glue a HomeLink to the back of each banner.

> **HomeLink:** Matthew 2:13-15, 19-23
>
> This banner uses Egyptian "picture-words" (hieroglyphics) to spell out the name "Jesus." Use this story throughout the week to help your child remember the Bible story.
>
> **An angel told Joseph to take Jesus to Egypt to keep Him safe from a bad king. Let's pack!** Roll arms twice, then clap hands. **It was a long way to Egypt!** Walk around the house. **Joseph, Mary, and Jesus were safe in Egypt. In another dream, an angel told Joseph it was safe to go back to the land of Israel. Let's pack!** Roll arms twice, then clap hands. **It was a long way to go. Joseph, Mary, and Jesus moved to the town of Nazareth.**

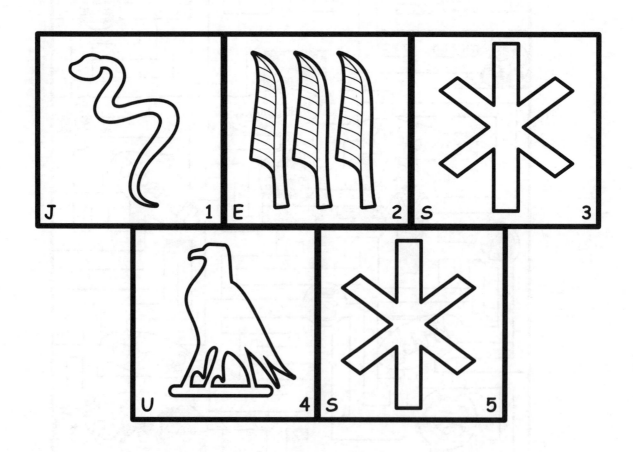

BCE19: Bible Bingo

Supplies: Photocopies of game card, pictures, and HomeLink · Colored pencils · Scissors · Glue · Five tokens per child (paper squares, dried beans, etc.) · Resealable plastic bags

Preparation: Photocopy the game card, picture squares, and HomeLink for each child. Also make one enlarged copy of the art to be used as the caller's game pieces.

Directions: The craft and game are combined today. Let each child color one set of pictures and cut them out. The children glue their pieces to a game card in any arrangement, as long as they are different from the other players. Glue a HomeLink to the back of each game card. Children may keep their game and playing pieces in a resealable plastic bag.

To play Bible Bingo, see page BS-43 in the Noah's Park *Snacks and Games Book*.

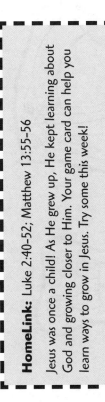

HomeLink: Luke 2:40-52; Matthew 13:55-56

Jesus was once a child! As He grew up, He kept learning about God and growing closer to Him. Your game card can help you learn ways to grow in Jesus. Try some this week!

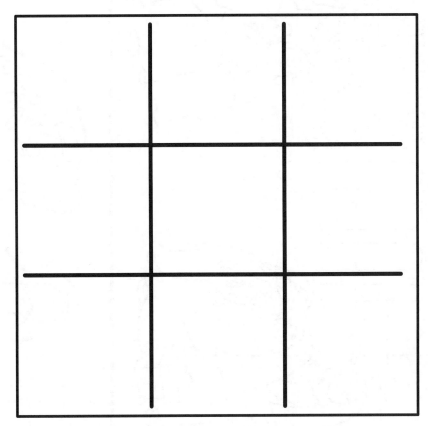

BCP19: Stick Puppets and Backdrop

Supplies: Copy of the puppets, backdrop, and HomeLink for each child · Colored pencils · Two craft sticks per child · Tape · Glue sticks · Resealable plastic bags

Preparation: Cut out a backdrop, the two puppets, and a HomeLink for each child.

Directions: Give each child a puppet of Jesus, a puppet of Mary and Joseph, and a backdrop to color. Help the children tape a craft stick to the back of each puppet. Help each child glue a HomeLink to the back of a backdrop. Show the children how to fold the backdrop on the dotted lines so that it stands. Send the pieces home in a resealable plastic bag.

HomeLink: Luke 2:40-52; Matthew 13:55-56

Help your child to use the stick puppets and backdrop to act out the Bible story this week.

Mary, Joseph, and Jesus went on a trip to Jerusalem. Many friends and family members went with them. They went to the temple to worship God for a special holiday. Mary and Joseph started home. They thought Jesus was with their group. But Jesus wasn't with them.

Mary and Joseph went back to Jerusalem. They found Jesus in the temple. He was talking and listening to the teachers. Jesus said that He needed to learn about His Father in heaven. Then Jesus went home with Mary and Joseph until He finished growing up.

BCE20: Clay Dove

Supplies: Peanut butter play dough (two cups smooth peanut butter, two cups powdered milk, three tablespoons honey) or use store bought play clay or make the alternate recipe below · Cardboard squares

Preparation: Combine the peanut butter, powdered milk, and honey in a bowl and mix well with bare hands. If the dough is too sticky for crafting, add more powdered milk, one tablespoon at a time. You may let the children mix their own edible clay during snack time.

Directions: Using the edible dough or store-bought clay, children can craft a dove that reminds them of the dove that symbolized God's pleasure in the Bible story. When finished, the children can put their dove on a cardboard square, write their name on the cardboard and leave it on the table until time to go home. Or you may let the children eat their creation. While crafting, lead the children in discussing ways they can please God. Be sure to send home a HomeLink paragraph with each child.

HomeLink: Matthew 3:13-17; John 1:32-34

Jesus always pleased God, His heavenly Father. We can please our heavenly Father too. Talk with your mom or dad about ways you could do this. Think about things like these:

Keep learning about Jesus.

Talk over everything with Jesus

Be kind to other kids.

Honor your parents.

Once you and your parents have some ideas, pray about them together.

Play Dough Recipe

2 c. flour

1 c. salt

4 T. cream of tartar

1 pkg. unsweetened dry drink mix for scent and color

2 c. warm water

2 T. cooking oil

Stir over medium heat until mixture pulls away from sides to form a ball. Store in airtight container. (For eight to ten children.)

BCP20: John the Baptist Puppet

Supplies: Copy of the John the Baptist puppet pattern and HomeLink for each child · Lunch-size paper bag for each child · Scissors · Crayons · Glue sticks · Optional: tan or brown fabric scraps

Preparation: Make a copy of the puppet pattern and HomeLink for each child. Cut out the face and clothes. If you are using the optional fabric, cut pieces for John's clothes.

Directions: Have the children color their puppet pieces (or glue on fabric pieces). Show the children how to glue the puppet pieces to the bag. The HomeLink should be glued to the back of the puppet. Help the children "talk" their puppets by moving the flap of the bag with their fingers. Encourage the children to make their John the Baptist puppet tell about Jesus.

HomeLink: Matthew 3:13-17; John 1:32-34

God chose John the Baptist to prepare people's hearts for Jesus' coming. By His act of obedience in being baptized, Jesus pleased God. Encourage your child to use the puppet during the week to act out the Bible story:

"I am John the Baptist. I lived by the Jordan River. I told people about Jesus, God's Son. I told them to be sorry for the wrong things they had done.

"One day Jesus came to be baptized. The heavens opened up. God sent His Spirit to Jesus, looking like a dove. Then God spoke. He said, 'This is My Son. I am pleased with Him.' Jesus did everything to please God."

BCE21: Fisher Buttons

Supplies: Copies of the button and HomeLink · Cardstock · Scissors · Colored markers · Clear self-adhesive paper · Safety pins · Tape · Scissors

Preparation: On cardstock, make a copy of the button for each child. Cut out the buttons. Cut out squares of clear self-adhesive paper large enough to place over the button. (Optional: cut enough squares of self-adhesive paper so each child can also cover the back side of their button.

Directions: Give each child a button pattern to color. When finished, help the children peel the backing off a clear self-adhesive paper square and lay it over their button to protect it. Then have the kids trim the adhesive paper to match the button. Glue the HomeLink to the back of the button. If you choose to cover the back of the button, have the children apply the self-adhesive paper and trim it at this time.

Help the children attach a safety pin to the back of their buttons by sliding a piece of tape through the closed pin to adhere the side that doesn't open. Children should write their names on their pins and then pin them on.

HomeLink:
Luke 5:1-11;
Matthew 4:18-22

Do you ever go fishing for people? You can be like Peter in the Bible story—and fish for people—whenever you help your family and friends learn about Jesus.

Talk over with your parents what you know about Jesus. Then talk about who you could tell about the Savior.

BCP21: Stringer of Fish

Supplies: Copies of three fish and a HomeLink for each child · Washable markers · Children's safety scissors · Yarn · Tape · Resealable plastic bags

Preparation: Make copies of the fish and HomeLink for each child. Cut yarn into one-foot lengths.

Directions: When Peter and Andrew went fishing with Jesus, they caught a lot of fish in their nets. Let's color some fish. Give each child three fish to color. Encourage original patterns and creativity.

When the children are done coloring, have them cut out their fish. Don't worry about the children doing a perfect job of cutting! You may need to help younger children.

Tape each child's three fish to one length of yarn to make it look like a stringer of fish. Be sure the words are in the correct order—"Jesus Loves Me." Let each child place the fish and HomeLink in a resealable bag.

HomeLink: Luke 5:1-11; Matthew 4:18-22

Jesus called Peter and Andrew to follow Him. Use your child's fish and other props at home to act out the Bible Story with your child. You could use a couple of chairs for the fishing boat and a towel for the fishing net.

Peter and Andrew were cleaning their nets. Jesus asked Peter to row Him out from the shore. Jesus taught the people about God. When He was done, Jesus told Peter to go out further onto the lake. Jesus told Peter to let down his nets. When Peter brought in the net, it was so full of fish that it was breaking! Peter decided to follow Jesus and be His helper.

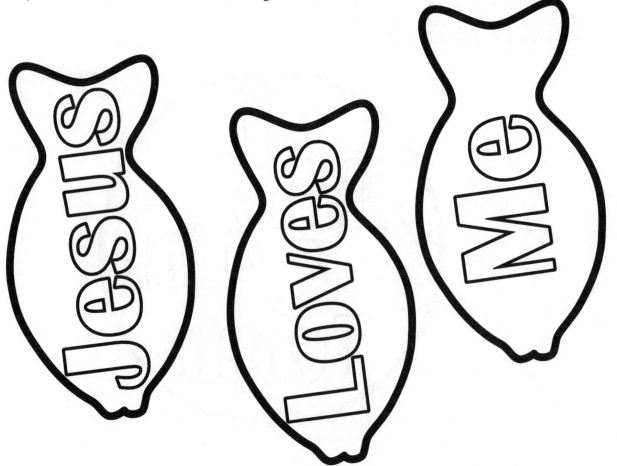

BCE22: Mini Mobiles

Supplies: Copies of the mobile pictures and HomeLink
· Colored pencils · Scissors · A pair of sharp scissors · Yarn
· Hole punch · Construction paper

Preparation: Make a copy of the five mobile pictures
and the HomeLink for each child. Cut yarn into 18"
lengths, one for each child. Cut yarn into 4" lengths, six
for each child. Cut construction paper into 6" x 9"
rectangles, one for each child.

Directions: Give each child a copy of the five mobile
pictures to color and cut out. Use a pair of sharp scissors
or a hole punch to make a small hole in the top and
bottom of each picture where indicated. Help the
children tie a 4" piece of yarn through the hole in the
top of each picture.

Fold the rectangular piece of construction paper like a
fan. With the hole punch, make three holes in the
construction paper as shown in the diagram. Using the 18"
piece of yarn, thread the yarn through the two outer holes
and tie the ends together at the top. The picture that says
"Jesus Cares" should hang from the middle hole of the "fan."
Tie the rest of the pictures to the holes in the bottom of the
other pictures. Tie the HomeLink to the last picture.

HomeLink: Mark 7:31-37

Jesus does good things. One of the good
things He does is care for our needs. How
does Jesus care for your needs? Talk it over
with your parents. Then pray with them
and thank Jesus for caring for you.
Remember to talk to Jesus about
your needs all week long.

BCP22: Bible Story Flannel Figures

Supplies: Copies of the flannel figures and HomeLink · Colored pencils · Felt · Glue sticks · Resealable plastic bags

Preparation: Copy a set of four flannel figures and a HomeLink for each child. Cut them out. Cut three 1" squares and one 2" square of felt for each child.

Directions: Give each child a set of figures to color. As the children work, talk about who the people were in the Bible story. Help the children glue a square of felt on the back of each figure. The 2" felt square should be glued to the back of the crowd figure. Send home each child's figures and a HomeLink in a resealable plastic bag.

> **HomeLink:** Mark 7:31-37
>
> Jesus did good things. One good thing He did was care for people's needs. Let your child stick the flannel figures to an upholstered chair or fuzzy blanket to retell the story while you play the following game.
>
> **Show me Jesus. Show me the people who brought the man to Jesus. Show me the man who couldn't hear or talk clearly. Jesus touched the man's ears. Show me your ears. Jesus touched the man's tongue. Show me your mouth. Show me the man after Jesus made him able to hear and talk.**

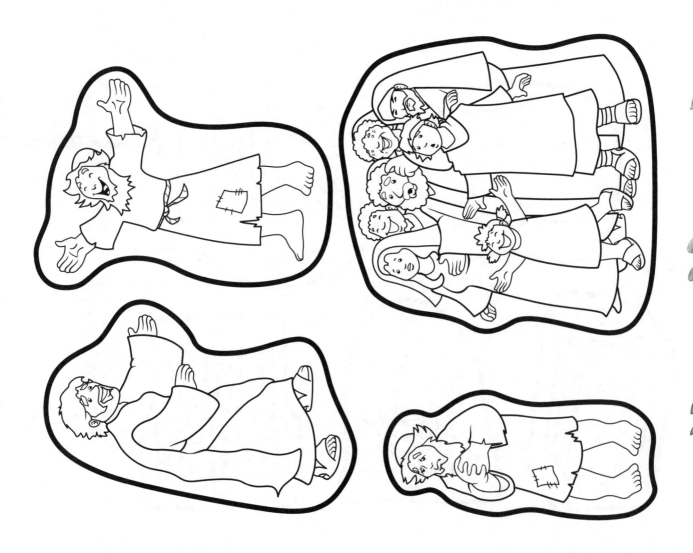

BCE23: Sheepish Ears

Supplies: Copies of the ear shape and HomeLink · Felt in a sheep color (brown, black, white) · Stiff white paper · Small cotton balls or batting · Glue · Tape · Stapler

Preparation: Copy the ear shape below onto cardboard; cut it out to use as a tracing pattern. Trace a pair of sheep ears on felt for each child. Cut stiff white paper into strips about 2" by 14". Copy a HomeLink for each child.

Directions: Give each child a strip of white paper to serve as a headband. Hold each child's band around their head to make it fit snugly and tape it. While waiting their turn, the children should glue cotton balls or batting on one side of a pair of ears. Help the children staple their ears onto their headbands.

As the children try out their Sheepish Ears, talk about how Jesus loves us as a shepherd loves his sheep. Be sure to send a HomeLink home with each child.

HomeLink: Luke 15:1-7

You are special to Jesus. He loves you very much. Jesus told the parable of the lost sheep to help us remember this.

Whenever you feel like you need a friend, make like a sheep and call on Jesus.

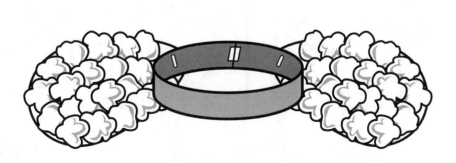

BCP23: Sheep Stand-up Figures

Supplies: Copies of the stand-up figures and HomeLink · Crayons · Resealable plastic bag

Preparation: Copy a set of figures and a HomeLink for each child. Cut them out.

Directions: Give each child a set of stand-up figures to color. As the children color, talk about Jesus' story of the lost sheep. Show the children how to fold the tabs on the sides of the figures on the dotted lines so that they stand up. Let each child put a set of figures and a HomeLink in a resealable plastic bag to take home.

HomeLink: Luke 15:1-7

Encourage your child to use the stand-up figures to act out the story:

Hide the sheep. Set up the rock and plant. Where is the shepherd? He had 100 sheep. One night, a sheep was missing. The shepherd looked for the sheep. He looked behind the rock. He looked behind the bush. Can you have the shepherd find the sheep? Jesus told this sheep story to teach us: God loves us as the shepherd loved the sheep.

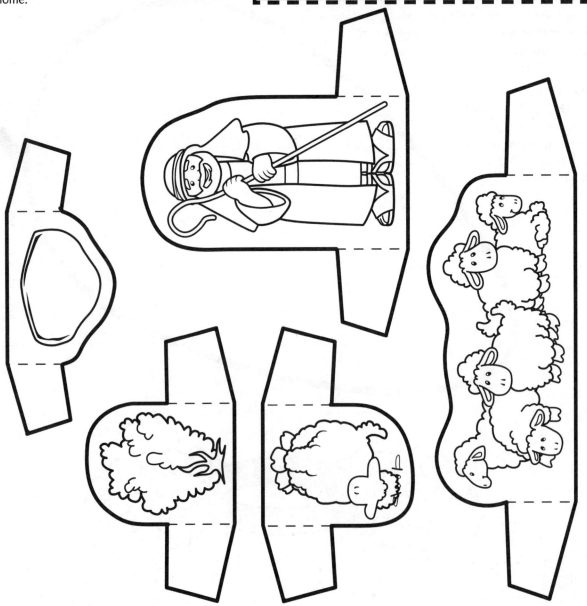

BCE24: Serving Coupons

Supplies: Copies of the coupons and HomeLink · Colored pencils · Scissors · Envelopes or resealable plastic bags

Preparation: Make copies of the coupons so that each child has six coupons. Also make a copy of the HomeLink for each child.

Directions: Give each child the Serving Coupons and read the words aloud. Explain how a coupon works: The children choose a way to serve someone, write it on the coupon, and give it to the person. When the person gives it back to them, that's when the child does the service they promised.

Brainstorm a variety of ways children can help at home, school, church, or elsewhere. Encourage the children to be realistic for their age level. Ideas might include helping a sibling with their chores, doing an extra chore for a parent or teacher, giving up some free time to help a coach or teacher, or doing something special for someone who's sick.

Have the children fill out the coupons with the service of their choice. Let the children know they can have six coupons and to use some of their other good ideas on some more. Allow time for the children to fill out their coupons, cut them out, and color them. Give each child a HomeLink to take home as well. Give them an envelope or resealable plastic bag for the coupons and HomeLink.

HomeLink: Mark 10:35-45; Matthew 20:17-28

Jesus taught us to serve us. He didn't give out Serving Coupons, but He was the perfect servant. He always showed God's love by helping others and putting them first.

Remember to give out your Serving Coupons as soon as you can. Show them to a parent before you give them out. Then remember to be cheerful when it's time to serve!

BCP24: Helper Bookmarks

Supplies: Copies of the bookmark pattern and HomeLink · Stiff paper (colorful, if possible) · Scissors · Clear self-adhesive paper · Washable markers

Preparation: Copy the bookmarks onto stiff paper, one for each child, and cut them out. Also copy the HomeLink. Cut a piece of clear self-adhesive paper, 8" x 5", for each child.

Directions: Give each child a bookmark to color. Read the bookmark to the children while they are coloring. Glue a HomeLink to the back of each bookmark. When finished coloring, fold the prepared clear self-adhesive paper in half. Take off the backing and set the bookmark on one half. Fold over the other half, sealing all the edges. Trim the edges to 1/4".

HomeLink: Mark 10:35–45; Matthew 20:17–28

Sometimes good things come in teaching. That's what happened in this week's Bible story. Jesus did a good thing by teaching His helpers to serve others. Encourage your child to find ways to serve and help others this week. Use the following story to review what Jesus taught.

Jesus and His helpers walking to Jerusalem. Pat your knees. **They stopped to rest.** Sit down. **The mother of James and John asked Jesus if they could have important places in heaven.** Pat the ground next to you. **Jesus taught them to serve and help others. What can you do to help someone?**

BCE25: Friendship Bracelet

Supplies: Copies of the patterns and HomeLink · Craft foam · Cardboard · Scissors · Sticky-backed hook and loop fasteners · Craft glue · Colored markers

Preparation: Copy the patterns onto cardboard and cut them out. Then trace the patterns onto craft foam, one bracelet for each child. Also trace the shapes onto foam, several for each child, and cut them out. Cut sticky-backed hook and loop fasteners into 3/4" squares. Make a copy of the HomeLink on regular paper for each child.

Directions: Remind the children that Jesus wants to forgive them and be their friend. Encourage them to wear a "friendship bracelet" during the week to remind them of this.

Measure a craft foam bracelet around each child's wrist and cut it to fit, leaving about a 3/4" - 1" overlap. Help the children peel the back off a square of sticky-backed hook and loop fasteners and stick it on the overlapping bracelet ends so that it holds together.

The children should unhook their hook and loop fasteners and lay their bracelets flat to glue on shapes of their choice. They may also draw pictures with marker. Encourage the children to choose shapes and pictures that remind them of Jesus' forgiveness. Also have the kids include their initials somewhere on their bracelet. Send a HomeLink home with each child.

> **HomeLink:** Luke 7:36-50
>
> Jesus forgives us when we do wrong. Like the woman in the Bible story, you can go to Jesus and say you're sorry. Jesus will always love you. Jesus will forgive you.
>
> This week, wear your Friendship Bracelet to remind you that Jesus wants to forgive you and be your Friend.

BCP25: Bible Story Poster

Supplies: Copies of the picture and HomeLink · Washable markers · Glue sticks · Construction paper

Preparation: Copy the picture and HomeLink for each child. As an option, you may enlarge the picture a little so that it's more like a poster.

Directions: Give each child a picture to color. Talk about what is happening in the picture. When finished coloring, help them make a matte for their pictures by gluing them onto construction paper. Glue a HomeLink to the back of each poster.

HomeLink: Luke 7:36-50

Jesus forgives us when we do wrong. Review the Bible story during the week by playing a game of "I Spy" with the Bible Story Poster. Have your child point to things in the picture that you "spy":

I spy Jesus sitting at Simon's table. I spy a woman who did bad things. I spy the woman's hair she used to wipe Jesus' feet. I spy the perfume the woman put on Jesus. I spy how happy the woman was when she was forgiven.

BCE26: Help! Doorknob Hanger

Supplies: Copies of the doorknob hanger and HomeLink · Cardstock or craft foam · Scissors · Colored markers · Other art supplies on hand (glitter glue, stickers, etc) · Glue

Preparation: Photocopy the doorknob hanger pattern and use it to trace and cut out the pattern on the cardstock or craft foam. Also copy the HomeLink for each child.

Directions: On the doorknob hanger, have the children write their names and glue the HomeLink on the back. Then have the children use glitter glue or other supplies to decorate the words "Ask God for Help!" Finally, ask the kids to decorate the rest of the doorknob hangar with colored markers and available craft supplies.

Encourage the kids to hang their Doorknob Hangers on their bedroom door at home as a reminder to pray all week long.

HomeLink: Matthew 7:7-8; Luke 6:12-16; John 17:20

Jesus teaches us to ask God for help. We can talk to God about everything! Show your Doorknob Hanger to your parents. Tell them what Jesus taught about prayer. Then hang it where it will remind you every day to talk to God.

BCP26: Prayer Pouch

Supplies: Copies of the cards and HomeLink · Crayons · A letter-sized envelope for each child · Yarn · Tape · Scissors · Decorative stickers

Preparation: Copy and cut out a set of cards and a HomeLink for each child. Cut a 12" length of yarn for each child.

Directions: Give each child the "Family" card. Have the kids draw a picture of their family on the card. Then hand out the "Friends" card, and let the children draw pictures of their friends. Repeat the drawing process with the "Sick People" cards and the "People at Church" cards.

When finished coloring, show the children how to tape one end of the yarn on each end of the envelope to use as a hanger. Glue a HomeLink to each envelope. Let the children decorate their envelopes with stickers.

> **HomeLink:** Matthew 7:7-8; Luke 6:12-16; John 17:20
>
> Jesus teaches us to ask God for help. Each day, let your child choose a card from the prayer pouch. Talk about people drawn on the card. You may want to use the following to begin the prayer time.
>
> **The Bible tells us that Jesus prayed. He prayed before He chose His helpers. He prayed for you and me. Jesus told us to pray. He told us to ask God when we need help. Let's pray today for** (name people shown on one of the cards).

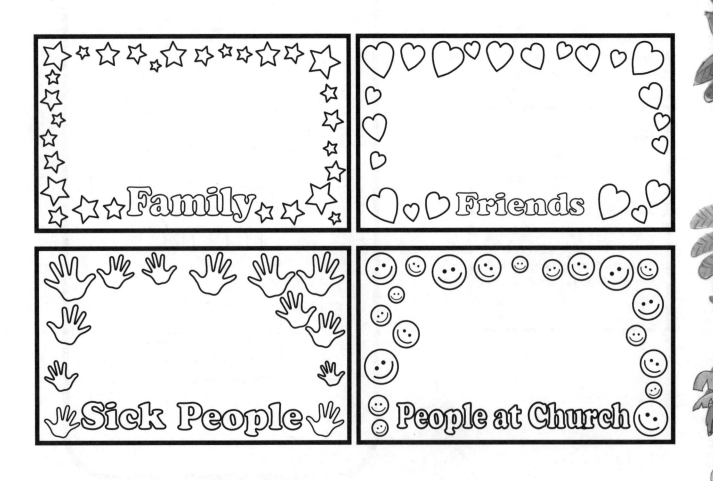

BCE27: Mosaic Wall Hanging

Supplies: Copies of the mosaic outline and HomeLink · Tissue paper in various colors · Scissors · Glue · Markers · Construction paper · Hole punch · Yarn

Preparation: Make a copy of the mosaic outline and HomeLink for each child. Cut tissue paper into shapes (rectangles, triangles, etc.) about a half-inch in size. Pour a little glue on paper plates for the kids to share.

Directions: Give each child a copy of the mosaic outline, and read it together. Set the tissue paper squares and paper plates of glue where all can reach them.

Show the kids how to dab a bit of glue onto the letters and then lightly touch a tissue paper shape to the letter. It's okay if part of the tissue paper sticks up. Do several pieces overlapping to create a multicolor mosaic. Then let the kids choose their colors and begin filling in all their letters in the word "Jesus." They can use markers to decorate the rest of the words.

When finished, help the kids each glue their mosaic to a piece of construction paper to form a stiff background and border. Have each child glue a HomeLink to the back. Punch two holes at the top and tie a piece of yarn through so the mosaic picture can be hung.

HomeLink: John 1:35-42; Matthew 16:13-17

Jesus is God's Son. Peter was the first of Jesus' helpers to figure this out. God helped him know it was true!

Show your mosaic picture to your parents. Then hang it where it will remind you that Jesus is God's Son.

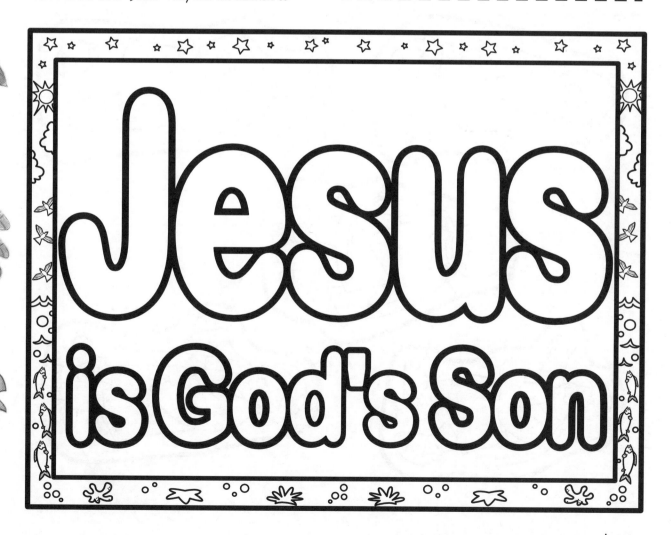

BCP27: Magnetic Bible Figures

Supplies: Copies of the Bible figures and HomeLink · Colored pencils · Magnetic tape · Scissors · Resealable plastic bags · Optional: cardstock

Preparation: Copy a set of the five figures and a HomeLink for each child. Cut them out. As an option, copy the figures onto cardstock to make them more sturdy. Cut five 1-inch lengths of magnetic tape for each child.

Directions: Give each child a set of five Bible figures. Talk about who they are as the children color. When done, help the children put a piece of magnetic tape on the back of each figure. Send home each child's figures and a HomeLink in a resealable plastic bag.

HomeLink: John 1:35-42; Matthew 16:13-17

We can know that Jesus is God's Son. Let your child use the magnetic figures on a cookie sheet or refrigerator door to retell the story. You may want to use the following "Guess Who" game to help your child remember the story:

Guess who said to Andrew and his friend, "Look! There is God's Son!" *(John the Baptist.)* **Guess who said, "Peter, I have found God's Son! Come and see!"** *(Peter's brother Andrew.)* **Guess who said, "Who do people think I am?"** *(Jesus.)* **Guess who said, "I know! You are God's Son."** *(Peter.)*

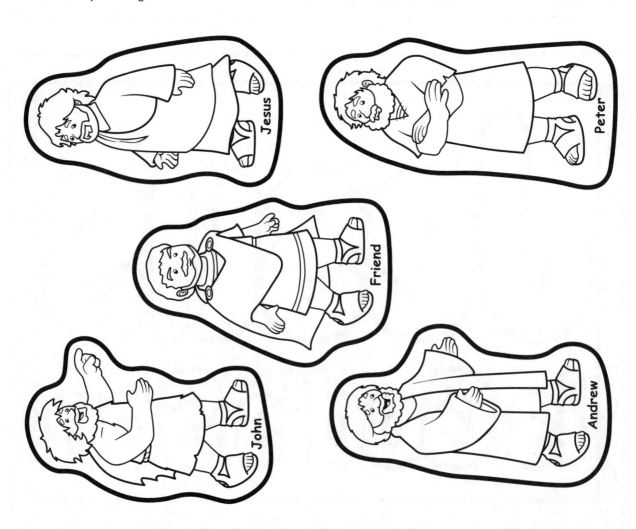

BCE28: Prayer Mural

Supplies: Butcher paper · Masking tape · Colored markers or crayons · Construction paper · Scissors · Glue · Copies of the HomeLink

Preparation: Tape a long length of butcher paper to a wall. Draw on it a simple background of a neighborhood, such as the outlines of a house, a school, and a playground. Title it: "Jesus Prays for Us." Make a copy of the HomeLink for each child.

Directions: Show the children the mural or bulletin board, and explain that Jesus prays for them and loves them no matter where they are. Tell the kids that they will add themselves to the mural.

Give out paper, markers, and scissors. Let the kids each create a picture of themselves, color it, and cut it out. Help the kids use a little glue to attach their picture to the mural wherever they choose. You may want to label the picture with the kids' names.

Be sure to send a HomeLink home with each child.

HomeLink: John 17:6-25; Hebrews 7:24-25

Jesus prays for us because He loves us! Everywhere you go, every day, Jesus loves you and prays for you.

Invite your parents to come see the mural that your children's church class made. Show them which picture is yours, and remind your parents that Jesus prays for them!

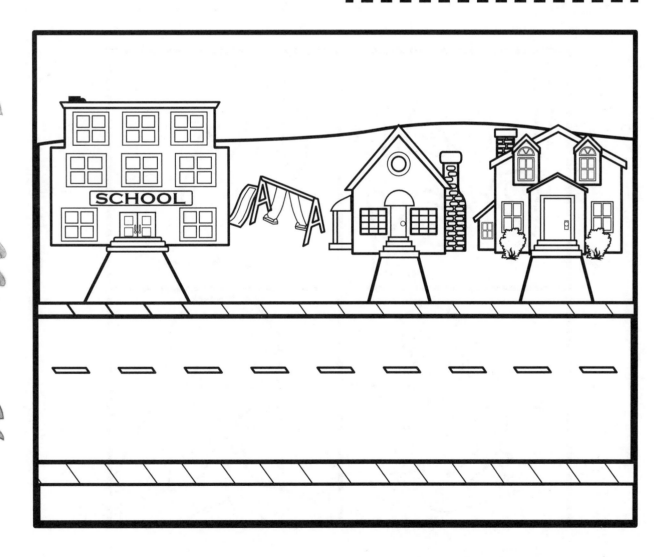

BCP28: Prayer Box

Supplies: Copies of the pictures and HomeLink
· Small cardboard box or berry basket for each
child · Scissors · Colored pencils · Glue

Preparation: Copy the four pictures and a
HomeLink for each child, and cut them apart.

Directions: Give each child the four pictures to
color. Talk about how the pictures can remind the
children that Jesus prays for them and that they
can pray for others. Help the children glue a
picture to each side of their box. Glue the
HomeLink to the bottom of the box.

**At home, put pictures of people you want
to pray for in your box. When you pray, pull
out a different picture each time and pray
for that person.**

HomeLink: John 17:6-25; Hebrews 7:24-25

Jesus prays for us because He loves us. Your child's Prayer
Box can be a reminder that Jesus prays for him or her. It can
also help your child pray for others. After reviewing the
Bible story with your child, spend time together drawing
pictures of people to pray for. Put them in the box. During
prayer times this week, let your child pick out pictures of
people to pray for.

**Jesus prayed. He prayed that His helpers would be
safe and full of joy. Jesus prayed. He prayed that
His helpers would learn through His Word and also
learn to love each other. Jesus prayed. He prayed
for people today who love Him. That's you!**

BCE29: Power Tools

Supplies: Children's modeling clay or homemade clay using the recipe below · Copies of the HomeLink · Waxed paper · Cardboard squares · Pencil · Optional: pictures of various power tools

Preparation: If you wish to make your own clay, prepare the recipe below in advance. Cut pieces of waxed paper for the children to use as a work mat. Cut 6" x 6" squares of cardboard to place the tools on to dry and take home.

Directions: Earlier we talked about Jesus' strong power being like a power tool. Let's each create our own "power tool" to remind us of Jesus' power.

Give each child a piece of waxed paper to use as a work mat and a handful of clay. Let the children handle and knead the clay as you talk about different kinds of power tools that could remind them of Jesus' power. (Some examples might be: power drill, power saw, power screwdriver, power sander, etc.) Help with ideas as needed. If you have pictures of power tools, have these available for the children to look at as they work. Be sure to send a HomeLink home with each child's power tool.

HomeLink: Mark 5:21-24, 35-43; Matthew 9:18-19, 23-26; Luke 8:40-42, 49-56

Who has power? Jesus! He has the power to help you. Whenever you need help this week, stop and talk to Jesus about it. Then look for how He sends you help.

Play Dough Recipe

2 c. flour

1 c. salt

4 T. cream of tartar

1 pkg. unsweetened dry drink mix for scent and color

2 c. warm water

2 T. cooking oil

Stir over medium heat until mixture pulls away from sides to form a ball. Store in airtight container. (For eight to ten children.)

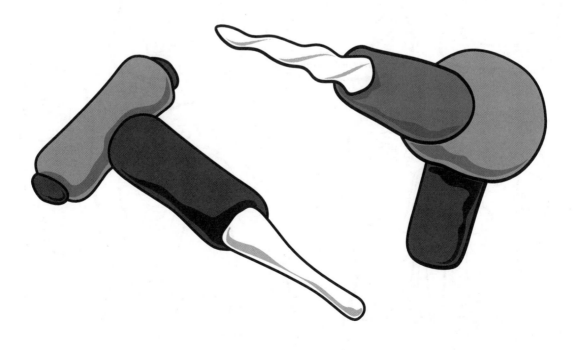

BCP29: Bible Story Stick Puppets

Supplies: Copies of the puppets and HomeLink · Crayons · Six craft sticks for each child · Tape · Resealable plastic bags

Preparation: Copy a set of six puppets and a HomeLink for each child, and cut them out.

Directions: Give each child a set of six puppets to color. As the children color, talk about who the puppets are and what they did in the Bible story. When finished, help the children tape a craft stick to the back of each puppet. Place the puppets and a HomeLink in a resealable bag for each child.

HomeLink: Mark 5:21-24, 35-43; Matthew 9:18-19, 23-26; Luke 8:40-42, 49-56

Jesus uses His power to help us! Let your child use the stick puppets to act out the following Bible story play:

Jesus was visiting a town. A man named Jairus came to Jesus. Jairus asked Him to make his little girl well. Jesus, His helpers, and Jairus started walking to Jairus's house. Some servants found Jairus and told him his little girl had died. Jesus told Jairus to trust Him. Jesus took His helpers, Jairus, and the girl's mother to the room where the girl was. Jesus held her hand and told her to get up. The little girl stood up. Jesus' power had made her alive again!

Jesus

Little Girl's Mother

Jairus

Helpers

Servants

Little Girl

BCE30: Instruments of Praise

Supplies: Copies of the HomeLink · Materials for the instrument(s) of your choice: 1. blocks of wood, sandpaper, duct tape or electrical tape; 2. eight-inch long dowel rods, colored markers; 3. small plastic or foam cups, beans, clear or decorative tape, stickers

Preparation: Choose which instrument(s) you'd like the children to make, and gather those supplies. If you choose to make all three instruments, arrange them as centers and divide the children among the three areas. Make a copy of the HomeLink for each child.

Directions: Tell the children what their instrument choices are, and walk them through the directions step by step. When finished, give each child a HomeLink to take home with their instrument.

Sandpaper Blocks—Cut wood into blocks about 3" square, two per child. Sand them well. Cut sandpaper into strips

3" x 5", one for every block.

Show the kids how to wrap the sandpaper around the edges of their blocks and securely tape them. The sand paper needs to be taped down tightly. Play the instrument by rubbing the sandpaper part of the blocks together.

Rhythm Sticks—Give each child two dowel rods to color. Instruct the children not to color the part they will hold as a handle so the color doesn't rub off on their hands. Play the instrument by tapping the sticks together.

Shakers—Give each child a small handful of beans to put in a cup. Have the children put another cup upside down over the first cup. Help the children securely tape the cups together. Children may use stickers to decorate the cups. Play the instrument by shaking the beans around.

HomeLink: Luke 19:29-38; John 12:12-19

We can praise Jesus our King! One way to praise Jesus is to make joyful music for Him. Use your instrument to try it this week. Play some praise music on a CD or cassette, and play your instrument along with it. You can march and sing too. You can even invite your family to join you. Let Jesus know you're happy that He's your King!

BCP30: 'Jesus Is King' Picture

Supplies: Copies of the picture and HomeLink · Colored markers · Fabric scraps · Glue · Construction paper

Preparation: Make a copy of the picture and HomeLink for each child. Cut the scraps of material into pieces no larger than 1 1/2" squares

Directions: Give each child a picture to color. When done, let the children glue fabric scraps on the road for coats. Mount each picture on construction paper. Glue a HomeLink to the back of each picture.

HomeLink: Luke 19:29-38; John 12:12-19

We can praise Jesus our King! Let your child help choose a place to hang this picture. Review the Bible story with your child during the week. Pat your knees whenever you read, "walk, walk" or "clippity, clop."

Walk, walk. Jesus was going to Jerusalem. Walk, walk. Two of Jesus' helpers brought Him a donkey. Clippity, clop. Jesus rode the donkey into Jerusalem. Clippity, clop. Some people put their coats on the road. Other people waved palm branches. "Hosanna, hosanna!" That's what people shouted. "Praise Jesus the King!"

BCE31: Colorful Cross

Supplies: Copies of the HomeLink · White cardboard or poster board · Scissors · Hole punch · Pencils · Tissue paper in many colors · Glue · Paper plates · Yarn or ribbon

Preparation: Make a copy of the HomeLink for each child. From cardboard or poster board, cut cross shapes about 6" x 4-1/2", with wide bars. Make one for each child. Punch a hole in the top of each. Cut tissue paper into two-inch squares. Pour a little glue onto paper plates for the kids to share.

Directions: Have each child glue a HomeLink to the back of a cross and write their name. Tie a length of yarn or ribbon through the hole for hanging. Then turn the crosses over to the front, and show the kids how to crumple a tissue paper square into a little ball, lightly dip it in glue, and press it onto the cross. It's okay if the balls come open a little. Caution the children to use only a tiny bit of glue so the picture will dry more quickly. The children should use lots of tissue paper balls and completely fill their crosses, pushing the balls close together, to make it colorful and give it a three-dimensional look. Allow the crosses to dry flat before moving.

> **HomeLink:** Luke 23:46—24:12; 1 Corinthians 15:4-5
>
> Jesus is God's special Son. Because He loves us, He died on the cross for our sins. But He rose from the dead. Many people saw Him. The Bible tells us it's true. And it's great news—Jesus will always be alive!
>
> Hang your cross where it will remind you that Jesus is alive. Talk with one of your parents about this good news.

BCP31: Butterfly Clip

Supplies: Copies of the butterfly pattern and HomeLink · Crayons · Spring-style clothespins · Glue · Marker

Preparation: Copy the butterfly and HomeLink for each child, and cut them out.

Directions: Give each child a butterfly, and read what it says on the wings. Let the children color their butterflies. Encourage them to color both the tops and backs of the wings.

Show the children how to fold the wings up so that the butterfly looks as if it were flying. Help the children glue the butterflies to a long straight end of a clothespin. Clip a HomeLink in each butterfly clothespin. Use a marker to print each child's name on the bottom of the clothespin.

HomeLink: Luke 23:46—24:12; 1 Corinthians 15:4-5

We can believe that Jesus is alive! The Butterfly Clip can remind your child of this truth. Review the Bible story with your child during the week.

Some people put Jesus on a cross, and there He died. Jesus let them do this. Joseph put Jesus' body in a cave-tomb. He put a big stone in front of the opening.

On Sunday morning, some women went back to the cave-tomb. The stone was rolled away! Where was Jesus? Two angels told them, "Jesus is alive!"

The women told Jesus' friends, "Jesus is alive!"

Peter went to see for himself. It was true! Later, Jesus appeared to Peter and the others. Jesus is alive!

BCE32: Potted Plants

Supplies: Copies of the HomeLink · Clear plastic cups · Permanent marker · Potting soil · Tablespoons · Water in a pouring container · Plant cuttings or seeds that grow quickly and easily (such as philadendron cuttings or pumpkin seeds) · Plastic wrap · Rubber bands · Newspaper · Paper towels · Optional: decorative stickers

Preparation: Copy the HomeLink for each child. Use permanent marker to label the cups with the children's names. If possible, plant a cutting or seed several weeks ahead of time so the children can see the sprout as an example. (Option: bring a plant that you already have growing that the children can see.)

Directions: Make three stations for the children, and have Park Patrol helpers at each. Cover each station with newspaper, and have paper towels on hand for cleanup.

Station 1: The children put potting soil in a cup with a spoon. Caution them not to fill the cup too full of soil. Leave plenty of room for the water and seeds.

Station 2: The children put a seed or cutting in their cup. Be careful the seeds don't get pushed down too deeply in the dirt because the sprouting will take a long time. If you are using plant cuttings, show the kids how to gently push aside the soil so the roots reach down in the cup.

Station 3: The children water their seeds or cuttings. Too much water will slosh out and make a muddy mess on the way home. If using seeds, put a piece of plastic wrap over the top of the cup and secure it with a rubber band. This creates a greenhouse effect, making an easy-care environment for the seeds to sprout in.

Since the children will have to wait their turn to go through the three stations, try ideas like these to keep them occupied: 1. Have a Noah's Park helper use a puppet to lead a game of "I Spy." 2. Children who have finished could decorate their pots with stickers.

Be sure each child takes a copy of the HomeLink with his or her plant when he or she leaves your classroom.

HomeLink: Genesis 1:11-12; 2:9a

God gives us a wonderful world. And part of His world is plants. There are so many, and they do so much! Grab a parent this week and go for a prayer walk together. Thank God for the plants you see as you walk.

Remember to take care of your seed or cutting over the next few weeks. Keep the soil damp but not muddy. The plastic wrap will help keep the moisture in. Once the seedling grows big enough to touch the plastic wrap, you can take it off. But remember to keep watering your seed or cutting!

BCP32: Flower Pinwheel

Supplies: Copies of the pinwheel pieces and HomeLink · Cardstock or stiff paper · Markers · Unsharpened pencils with erasers · Straight pins · Tape · Small dot stickers · Glue

Preparation: Make copies of the pinwheel and leaves on cardstock or stiff paper. Cut them out. Also copy the HomeLink. Assemble a pinwheel in advance to see how it goes together.

Directions: Give each child a pinwheel and two leaves to color. When finished, help the children assemble their pinwheels: Fold tab 1 to the center dot, matching the dots. *Don't crease the cardstock; just bend it over.* Do the same for tabs 2, 3, and 4 in order. Stick a straight pin through all four tabs and the center dot. This forms the petals. Push the pin into the eraser portion of the pencil (in the side). Allow space on the pin for the pinwheel to rotate. Put a small dab of glue on the eraser where the point of the pin sticks through to protect the children's fingers. The pencil forms the flower stem. Let each child put a small dot sticker on the head of the pin for the center of the flower. Finally, tape the leaves onto the pencil. Send home the flower pinwheel with a HomeLink.

> **HomeLink:** Genesis 1:11-12; 2:9a
>
> God gives us a wonderful world. And God filled His wonderful world with plants. Go outside with your child and the flower pinwheel to make it blow in the breeze. Then name all the different plants you and your child can see.

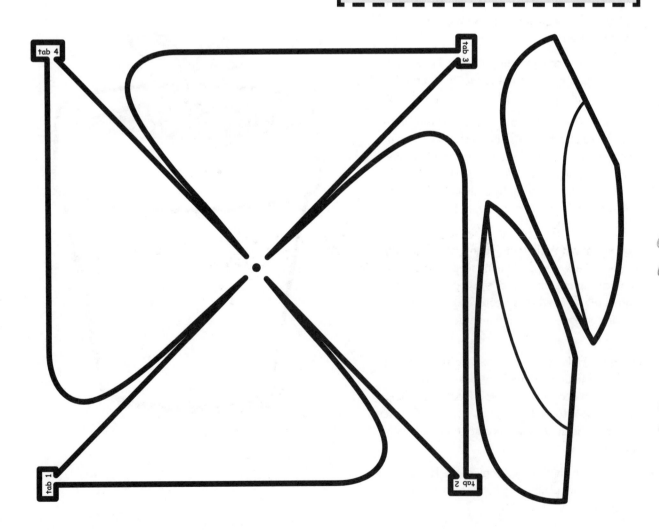

BCE33: Animal Sculpting

Supplies: Copies of the HomeLink · Clay or play dough · Cardboard squares · Plastic knives · Pencils

Preparation: Purchase or prepare play dough (see recipe on this page). Make a copy of the HomeLink for each child.

Directions: Let each child use a lump of clay or play dough to make an animal figure on a cardboard square. Encourage the children to experiment as they use their hands to sculpt an animal and a plastic knife to carve details. Have the kids use a pencil to write their names on their cardboard. The animal sculptures may dry at home during the week. Be sure to send a HomeLink home with each sculpture.

Play Dough Recipe

2 c. flour

1 c. salt

4 T. cream of tartar

1 pkg. unsweetened dry drink mix for scent and color

2 c. warm water

2 T. cooking oil

Stir over medium heat until mixture pulls away from sides to form a ball. Store in airtight container. (For eight to ten children.)

HomeLink: Genesis 1:20-25

God gave us a wonderful world. And He filled it with many different kinds of animals. Go on an "animal hunt" this week. Take a parent with you, and see how many different animals you can spot around your neighborhood. Pray together to praise God for making animals.

BCP33: Animal Matching Game

Supplies: Copies of the animal cards and HomeLink · Colored pencils · Scissors · Resealable plastic bags

Preparation: Make two copies of the six animal cards for each child. (Each child will need a pair of animals.) Copy one HomeLink for each child. If you have younger preschoolers, you may want to cut the cards apart before class.

Directions: Give each child a set of 12 cards to color (two of each animal). Encourage the children to color each pair of animal cards the same. Let the children cut the cards apart. After teaching the children how to play the matching game, place each child's cards and a HomeLink in a resealable plastic bag.

The Animal Matching Game is played like Concentration: Mix up one set of cards and place them face down in two rows. Turn up two cards at a time. If they match, set the pair aside. If they don't match, turn them back down again. Continue until all the animal pairs are found.

HomeLink: Genesis 1:20–25

God made all kinds of animals to fill the water, sky, and land. Play the Animal Matching Game with your child to reinforce the Bible story:

Lay out all the cards, picture-side down. Take turns turning over two cards at a time. If both cards match, say, "God made (name of the animal)," and remove that pair. Keep playing until all the animal pairs have been found.

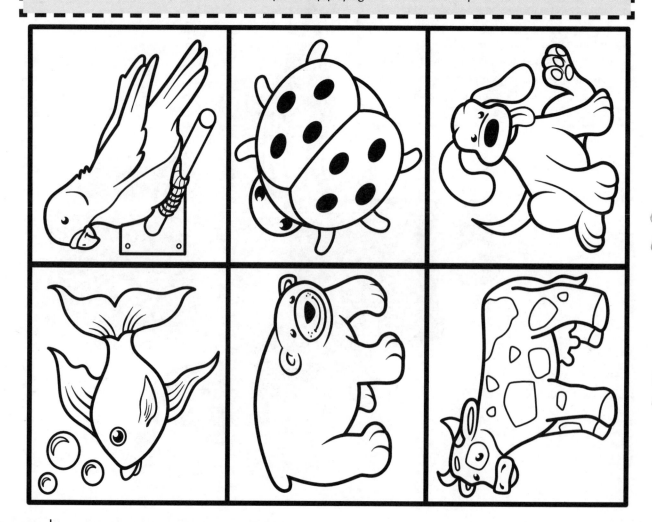

GCE34: Special People Maps

Supplies: Copies of the map and HomeLink · Scissors · Construction paper · Colored pencils · Glue · Plain white paper · Optional: camera that takes instant pictures

Preparation: Make a copy of the map and HomeLink for each child. Cut construction paper into 9" x 6" rectangles. Cut plain white paper into 2" squares. If you have access to an instant camera, plan to take each child's picture during the lesson to be added to the maps.

Directions: Give each child a copy of the map to color. When finished, the kids may glue their map to a construction paper rectangle to strengthen it and form a border. Help the children title their maps: "People Are God's Special Creation." The kids may write their names

on the back and glue a HomeLink on the back as well. To finish their maps, the children should each draw a picture of themselves on the plain paper squares (or use a photograph) and add it to North America.

HomeLink: Genesis 1:26-28; 2:18-22; Psalm 8

People are God's special creation. God made people in His likeness, to be like Him, to be His friends. All people are made in God's likeness—all the people of the world! That means you, too!

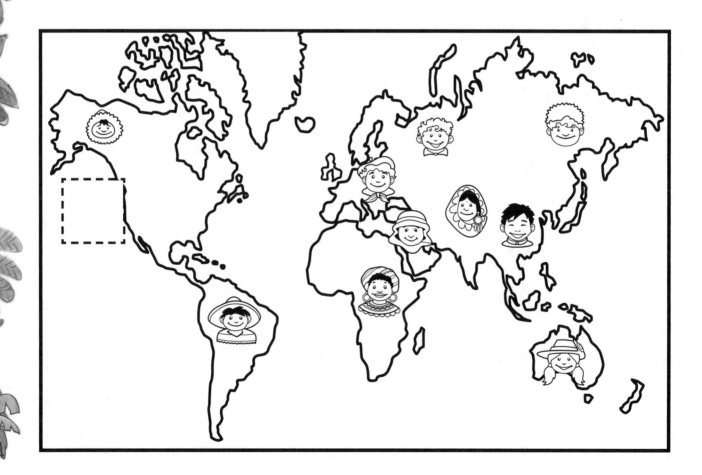

GCP34: Creation Picture

Supplies: Copies of the Creation Picture, Adam and Eve, and the HomeLink · Colored markers · Glue sticks

Preparation: Make a copy of the Creation Picture, Adam, Eve, and the HomeLink for each child. Cut the two slits in each picture. Cut out the Adam and Even figures so they are ready to use.

Directions: Give each child a Creation picture and Adam and Eve to color. Show the children how to slide Adam and Eve into the slits: Help each child glue a HomeLink on the back of the picture (avoiding the slits).

HomeLink: Genesis 1:26-28; 2:18-22; Psalm 8

God gives us a wonderful world. People are God's special creation. Use the Creation Picture to help your child review this truth during the week.

God gives us a wonderful world. What did He make? Have your child point to all the things God made. **After making all these things, God made something special. God made people. He made a man named Adam and a woman named Eve.** Have your child put the Adam and Eve figures in the slits. **God made people special. God made you special too!**

BCE35: 3-D Nature Picture

Supplies: Copies of the nature pictures and HomeLink · Colored pencils · Scissors · Stiff paper · Construction paper · Glue

Preparation: Make a copy of the five nature pictures and the HomeLink for each child. Cut stiff paper into strips 1" x 3" (5 per child). Make a sample 3-D picture so you can easily show the kids how to fold the pieces.

Directions: Give each child a set of five nature pictures to color and cut out. Give each child five paper strips to accordion fold. It's okay if the folds are not even. The kids glue one end of each folded strip to the back of a nature picture. Set them aside to dry for a minute.

Give each child a piece of construction paper. Show the kids how to fold each edge over about a half inch. The children may unfold the edges for now and then draw a simple background for a nature scene, leaving room for the five nature pictures. Have the kids title their scenes: "Take Care of God's Creation." They may glue a HomeLink to the back.

Have the kids go back to the folded edges of their construction paper and cut a diagonal in from the point, up to where the folds meet at each corner. This makes two pointed flaps at each corner. The kids refold the four sides, letting the flaps overlap and forming a shallow box. Have the kids glue the flaps in place.

Now the kids may glue the other end of their accordion-folded strips to their background to make the pictures pop out from it.

HomeLink: Genesis 1:26-31; 2:7-8, 15, 18-23

God wants people to care for His world. He put people in charge of all He made. How can you help take care of different parts of God's world? How can you responsibly use what God has made? Talk over some ideas with your parents.

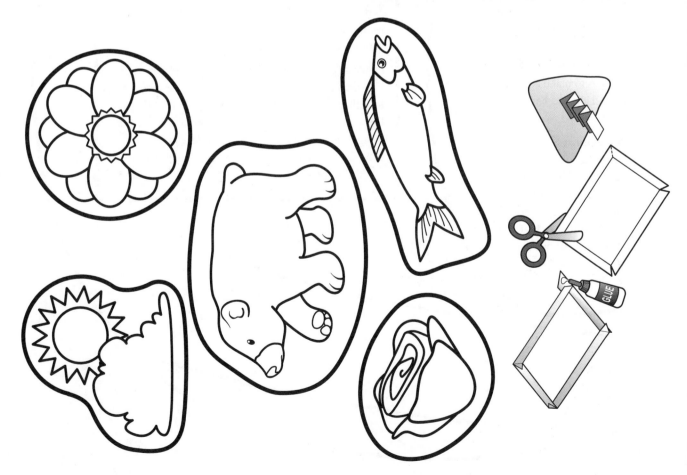

BCP35: Caring Keeper Visor

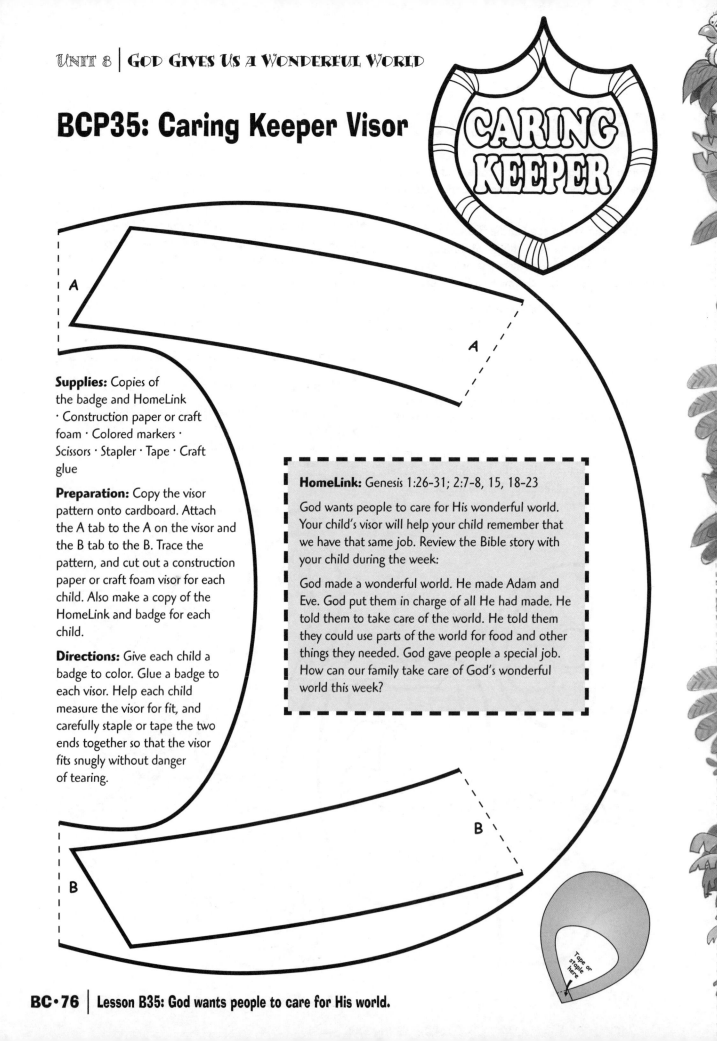

CARING KEEPER

A

A

Supplies: Copies of the badge and HomeLink · Construction paper or craft foam · Colored markers · Scissors · Stapler · Tape · Craft glue

Preparation: Copy the visor pattern onto cardboard. Attach the A tab to the A on the visor and the B tab to the B. Trace the pattern, and cut out a construction paper or craft foam visor for each child. Also make a copy of the HomeLink and badge for each child.

Directions: Give each child a badge to color. Glue a badge to each visor. Help each child measure the visor for fit, and carefully staple or tape the two ends together so that the visor fits snugly without danger of tearing.

HomeLink: Genesis 1:26-31; 2:7-8, 15, 18-23

God wants people to care for His wonderful world. Your child's visor will help your child remember that we have that same job. Review the Bible story with your child during the week:

God made a wonderful world. He made Adam and Eve. God put them in charge of all He had made. He told them to take care of the world. He told them they could use parts of the world for food and other things they needed. God gave people a special job. How can our family take care of God's wonderful world this week?

B

B

Tape or staple here

BCE36: Door Wreath

Supplies: Copies of the title circle and HomeLink · White paper plates · Hole punch · Yarn or ribbon · Craft glue · Hot glue gun · Scissors · A large variety of small craft supplies and nature items (whatever you have on hand or can easily get): fabric and felt scraps, craft foam shapes, pom-poms, beads, sequins, buttons, acorns, tiny seashells, twigs, sand, sunflower seeds, birdseed, dried beans, potpourri, dried flower petals, and even popped popcorn

Preparation: Copy and cut out the title circle and HomeLink for each child. Cut one 6" piece of yarn or ribbon for each child

Directions: Have each child glue a copy of the title circle to the center of a paper plate. Have the kids glue a HomeLink to the back. Help the children punch a hole in the top of their plate and tie a piece of yarn or ribbon through as a hanger.

Then let the children choose from an assortment of craft and nature items to glue around the edge of the plate to form a wreath. They should cover the whole bumpy part, about two inches wide.

You may need to use a hot glue gun on heavier or slicker items. *Do not let the kids touch the glue gun,* but do let them show you where on their wreath you should glue those items.

HomeLink: 2 Kings 4:8-13

God cares about where we live. He provided a special little spot for Elisha. He has also given you a special spot to live in—a spot where you can serve and thank Him. Talk with your parents about where you can hang your door wreath as a reminder.

BCP36: Home Sampler

Supplies: Copies of the sampler picture and HomeLink · Crayons · Construction paper · Glue

Preparation: Copy and cut out the Home Sampler and HomeLink for each child.

Directions: Give each child a sampler picture to color. Read what it says, and explain that these kinds of pictures are sometimes sewn with thread. Have each child glue their picture to a larger sheet of construction paper to make it look framed. Glue a HomeLink to the back of each picture.

HomeLink: 2 Kings 4:8-13

Everyone needs a place to live. And God cares about where we live. Help your child choose a good reminder spot to hang the Home Sampler. Review the Bible story together:

Elisha traveled to many towns telling people about God. He often went to a town called Shunem. There a woman and her husband made a room for Elisha. They put a bed, a table with a lamp, and a chair in the room. Elisha had a place to stay whenever he was in Shunem. God cares about where we live.

BCE37: Friendship Card

Supplies: Copies of the card pieces and HomeLink · Colored pencils · Scissors · Construction paper · Glue

Preparation: Make a copy of the card pieces and a HomeLink for each child.

Directions: Instruct the kids to each choose one good friend to make a card for. Give each child a set of card pieces, and ask the kids to choose which ones they'd like to put on their card. They don't need to use all of them, and they can draw other things on their card as well. Let the children color and cut out their symbols. Help the children also complete the sentence in the box and cut it out. Give each child a sheet of 9" x 12" construction paper to fold in half to form the card. The kids choose where to glue their chosen symbols and sentence. The

children may further decorate their cards as time permits. Give each child a HomeLink to take home with their card.

HomeLink: 1 Samuel 18:1-4; 19:1-7; 20:1-42

God wants us to be friends to others. David and Jonathan in the Bible story were a good example of friends. Talk with your parents about your friends. What are good ways to show friendship? How can you be friendly with other kids? If you need to, ask a parent to help you deliver the friendship card you made.

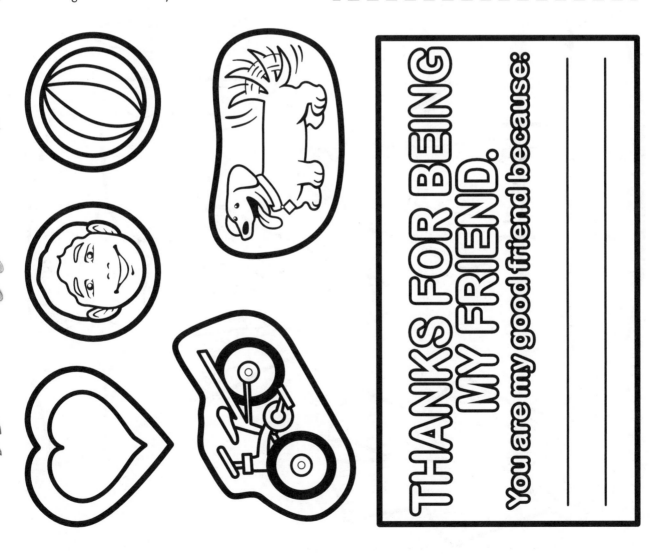

THANKS FOR BEING MY FRIEND. You are my good friend because:

BCP37: David and Jonathan Action Figures

Supplies: Copies of the figures and HomeLink · Cardstock or stiff paper · Colored pencils · Resealable plastic bags

Preparation: Copy the action figures and props onto cardstock or stiff paper, one set for each child. Cut them out. Also make a copy of the HomeLink for each child.

Directions: Give each child a set of figures to color. While coloring, talk about how David and Jonathan were friends. Show the children how to fold the tabs on David and Jonathan to make them stand. Place each child's figures and a HomeLink in a resealable plastic bag to take home.

HomeLink: 1 Samuel 18:1-4; 19:1-7; 20:1-42

God wants us to be friends to others. Help your child use the action figures to act out the story:

David was a brave young man. He lived at King Saul's palace. Jonathan was King Saul's son. David and Jonathan were very good friends. Jonathan gave David his coat, sword, and bow. Jonathan promised to always help David. David promised to always be a friend to Jonathan and his family.

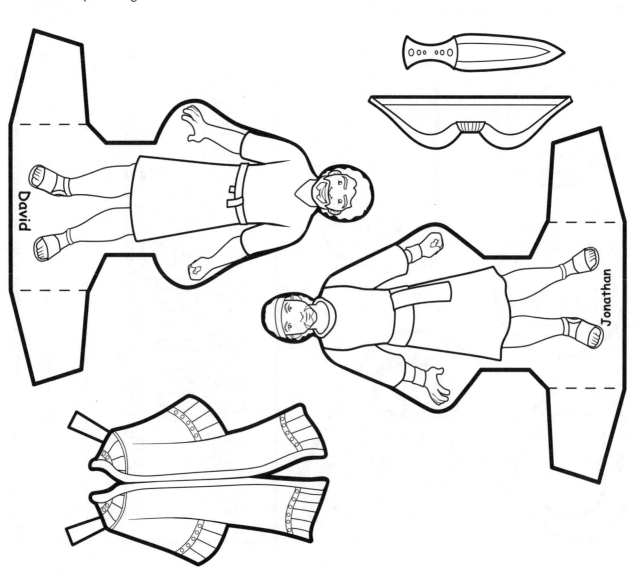

BCE38: Stand-up Bible Story Picture

Supplies: Copies of the Israelite picture and Homelink · Blue construction paper · Colored pencils or markers · Glue · Blue cellophane · Optional: fish stickers

Preparation: Copy the Israelite picture and HomeLink for each child. Cut cellophane into one-inch strips.

Directions: Give each child a picture of the Israelites to color. Give each child a piece of 9" x 12" blue construction paper. Help the children fold the construction paper in thirds. After folding, each section of the paper should be approximately 4" wide and 9" long. Have them glue their colored picture of the Israelites in the center section of the construction paper. As an option, the children may add stickers of fish on the blue "water" on either side of the Israelites.

Be sure the construction paper is unfolded for this next step: The children put a thin strip of glue along the top edge of both side-folds and place strips of cellophane on the glue to hang down. When the glue is dry the sides should be folded again so they stand up making this look like wavy water. The children may choose to cut the bottoms of the strips in different lengths. Now the picture looks like the Israelites are walking through the water on dry land.

HomeLink: Exodus 14:1-31

God can help us when we are afraid. Put your picture in a spot that will remind you of how God helped the Israelites. Tell one of your parents the story. Then pray together about what makes you afraid. Look for ways God helps you.

BCP38: Exodus Flannel Figures

Supplies: Copies of the figures and HomeLink · Scissors · Felt · Colored pencils · Glue · Resealable plastic bags

Preparation: Copy one set of figures and a HomeLink for each child. Cut them out. Cut five 1-inch squares of felt for each child.

Directions: Give each child a set of figures to color. Show the children how to glue a square of felt on the back of each figure. Send home each child's figures and a HomeLink in a resealable plastic bag.

> **HomeLink:** Exodus 14:1-31
>
> God can help us when we are afraid. Let your child stick the flannel figures to an upholstered chair or a fuzzy blanket to retell the story.
>
> **Here is Moses. Here are the Israelites. Moses is leading the Israelites out of Egypt to a new land. Here is the Red Sea. Here come the soldiers of Egypt. The Israelites are afraid! What did God do? He opened the Red Sea for Moses and the Israelites to cross. God closed the waters on the Egyptians. God helped the Israelites when they were afraid.**

Egyptians

Moses

Israelites

BCE39: Ten Rules Tablet

Supplies: Copies of the rules and HomeLink · Brown paper grocery bags · Scissors · Glue · Cardboard

Preparation: Copy the rules and a HomeLink for each child. Cut open brown paper grocery bags so they lie flat. Cut cardboard into strips 1" x 10".

Directions: Give each child a copy of God's Rules to cut out. Read the rules together. Have each child glue his or her rules on a piece of brown paper bag, leaving a border. Then show the kids how to cut around the tablet, about one inch wider on all sides, to make the brown paper have the same tablet shape.

The kids will each use a cardboard strip to form a stand for their tablet. Fold a strip of cardboard into a triangle, with the ends overlapping just enough to glue them together. One leg of the triangle is glued to the back of the tablet to form a stand. Glue a HomeLink to the back of the tablet above the stand.

HomeLink: Exodus 19:1-25; 20:1-17

God gives us rules in the Bible. They're good rules. They help us to be safe and happy. They help us know what's best.

Talk over God's rules with your parents. Which ones are easy for you? Which ones are hard? Pray together to ask God's helping with obeying His rules.

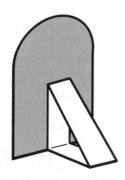

GOD'S RULES

I. PUT GOD FIRST

II. WORSHIP ONLY GOD

III. SPEAK GOD'S NAME KINDLY

IV. HAVE A DAY OF REST

V. HONOR YOUR PARENTS

VI. DON'T MURDER

VII. LOVE YOUR OWN HUSBAND OR WIFE

VIII. DON'T STEAL

IX. TELL THE TRUTH

X. DON'T WANT WHAT OTHERS HAVE

BCP39: God's Rules Cards

Supplies: Copies of the cards and HomeLink · Stiff paper · Hole punch · Crayons · Large paper clips

Preparation: Copy a set of five cards and the HomeLink for each child on stiff paper, and cut them out. Use a hole punch to make a hole as indicated in the top of each card.

Directions: Give each child the first card to read together and color. Continue to give out the cards one at a time for the children to color. Be sure to give them the HomeLink before proceeding with the next part of the activity. Then show the children how to straighten out the loose side of a paperclip. The kids slide each card onto the paper clip through the hole in the top of each card; then they push the card around the loop to the bottom. This forms a little key ring to hold the card set together. Help the children push the paper clip point back where it belongs.

HomeLink: Exodus 19:1-25; 20:1-17

God gives us rules. His rules show His love and care for us. During the week, use the cards with the following story to reinforce the lesson. The rules on the cards have been simplified.

God asked Moses to come to the top of a mountain. God met Moses there. God gave Moses rules for the Israelites. The rules showed the people that God loved them. Here are some of God's rules. Go over the cards, one at a time, with your child.

BCE40: Feathery Bird Reminder

Supplies: Copies of the bird and HomeLink · Construction paper · Scissors · Glue · Colored markers

Preparation: Make a copy of the bird and HomeLink for each child. Use the feather pattern to cut five or more feathers from construction paper for each child. As an option, you may copy the feather pattern onto construction paper and let the children cut out their own feathers during craft time.

Directions: Brainstorm together ways that God cares for the children in your class. Have the kids write an idea on each of their feathers. Park Patrol may help younger children. Let the kids glue their feathers to the side of a bird without the HomeLink and further color it. Read the HomeLink with the children to remind them to look for ways God provides for each of them.

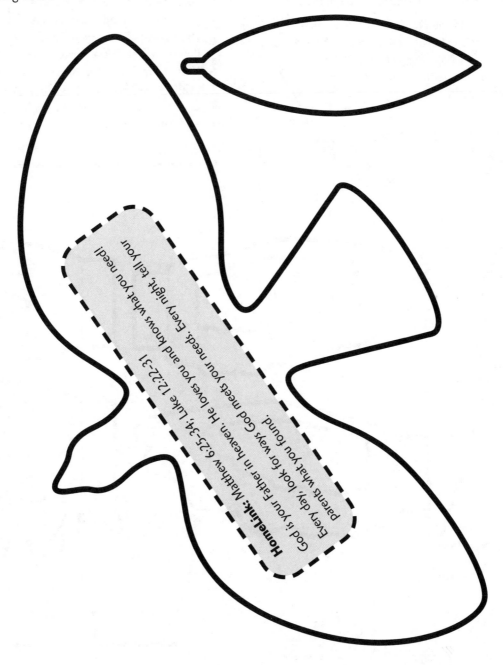

HomeLink: Matthew 6:25–34; Luke 12:22–31
God is your Father in heaven. He loves you and knows what you need! Every day, look for ways God meets your needs. Every night, tell your parents what you found.

BCP40: Bird and Flower Stick Puppets

Supplies: Copy of the puppet pieces and a HomeLink for each child · Two wide craft sticks per child (tongue-depressor size) · Crayons · Tape · Yellow chenille wire · Resealable plastic bags

Preparation: Cut out the puppet pieces and the HomeLinks. Each child needs one set of bird pieces and two sets of flowers. Cut two 2" lengths of chenille wire for each child.

Directions: Give each child the bird puppet parts to color. Help the children tape the tabs onto one of the craft sticks.

Then let each child color four flower halves. Help the children tape the tabs of two flower halves to each chenille wire to form two whole, floppy flowers. Then help the children tape the chenille stems to the end of the other craft stick.

Place each child's puppets and a HomeLink in a resealable plastic bag.

HomeLink: Matthew 6:25-34; Luke 12:22-31

Jesus used birds and flowers to illustrate that our heavenly Father loves us and knows what we need. Let your child use the puppets to reinforce the Bible story throughout the week.

Jesus said, **"Look at the birds."** "Fly" the bird puppet. **"God feeds them. And look at the flowers."** Have your child "smell" the flower puppet. **"The flowers are prettier than a king wearing his richest clothes,"** said Jesus. **"God dresses the flowers. God is your Father in heaven. He loves you and knows what you need."**

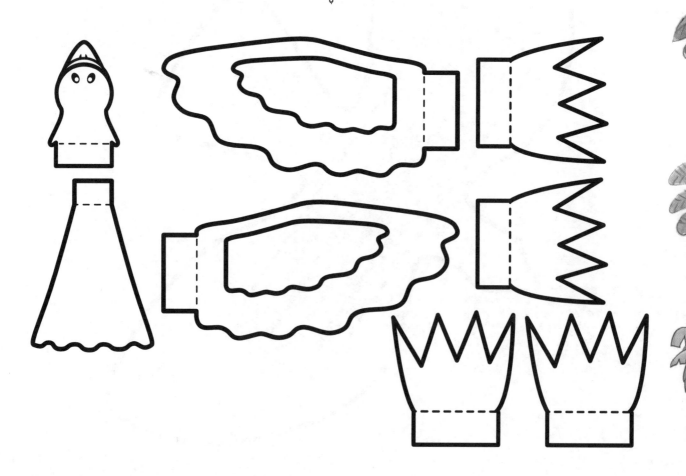

BCE41: Prayer Chains

Supplies: Construction paper · Markers · Scissors · Glue

Preparation: From a variety of colors, cut construction paper strips 1/2" x 6", seven per child.

Directions: Let each child choose seven strips of construction paper. On each strip, the kids write one of the days of the week. You may wish to write the words on the board for them to copy. When finished, the kids glue the end of the Sunday strip together to make a link. Then they loop the Monday strip through the Sunday link and glue it. Repeat until there is a seven-link chain in order.

Give each child a HomeLink and read it together. Then set aside the Prayer Chains and HomeLinks in a safe spot until the end of class.

HomeLink: Luke 11:1-4

Jesus taught us how to pray to our Father in heaven. He loves you so very much! Take time to talk with Him every day this week. Let your Prayer Chain remind you. After you pray each day, tear off the link with that day's name on it.

Some days you can pray with your parents or another relative. Some days you can pray with a friend. And some days you can pray alone—just you and your loving Father in heaven.

BCP41: Prayer Help Cards

Supplies: A copy of the six picture cards and HomeLink for each child · Crayons · Scissors · Envelopes

Preparation: Make a copy of the cards and a HomeLink for each child. Cut out the HomeLinks. If you have young children who have not yet begun using scissors, cut out the Prayer Help Cards for them.

Directions: Give a sheet of Prayer Help Cards to each child. Let the children color them. Talk about what the pictures mean. Then let the children cut their cards apart. Place each child's Prayer Help Cards and a HomeLink in an envelope.

HomeLink: Luke 11:1-4

Jesus taught His disciples what to include when they pray. Use these Prayer Help Cards to help your child pray the Lord's Prayer.

Picture 1–"Our Father."

Picture 2–"God is a great God." (Hallowed be your name)

Picture 3–"God, You're in charge." (Your will be done)

Picture 4–"Please give us what we need." (Give us this day our daily bread)

Picture 5–"We're sorry. Please forgive us." (Forgive us our sins)

Picture 6–"Help us do what we're told." (Lead us not into temptation)

BCE42: Jacob's Stairway

Supplies: Copies of the pictures below · Markers or crayons · Construction paper · Scissors · Glue

Preparation: Copy a set of the pictures (and title) below for each child.

Directions: Give each child a set of pictures, and talk about places children go where God is with them. Have the children color and cut out their pictures.

Let each child choose a sheet of 9" x 12" construction paper and fold the paper accordion style. On the back, have the kids glue the HomeLink to the top "step." Let the kids each cut two long strips from another sheet of construction paper, about 1/2" wide and 6" long. On the side with the HomeLink, the kids dot glue along both edges on the folds sticking up. Then they lay their strips on the glue. This forms a brace that will hold the folded paper in a stairway shape.

On the front side of the stair steps, the children may glue their pictures, along with the title. If time permits, they may also draw additional pictures, on extra paper, showing places they go during the week where God is with them.

HomeLink: Genesis 28:10-22

Where do you go every day? Where do you go now and then? Let this stairway remind you that God's promise to Jacob is good for you too. God promises to be with you wherever you go!

This week, see if you can retell the Bible story to your parents. Every day, think about God being with you.

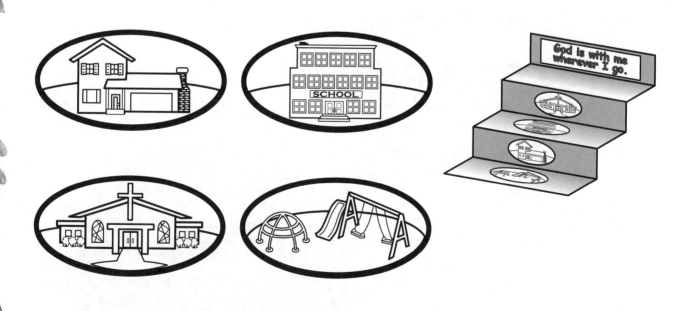

God is with me
wherever I go.

BCP42: Stone Reminder

Supplies: Copies of the "God loves me" oval and HomeLink · Crayons · One clean stone for each child (oval needs to fit on it) · White craft glue in containers · Paintbrushes · Waxed paper · Resealable plastic bags

Preparation: Make a copy of the oval and HomeLink for each child, and cut them out. Wash and thoroughly dry the rocks.

Directions: Give each child a piece of waxed paper to use as a placemat. Let the children each color a "God loves me" oval. Read the words together.

Help the children glue their oval to a rock. Then let the children "paint" a thin layer of glue over the top of the paper, overlapping onto the rock. Send the stones and a HomeLink home in a resealable plastic bag. Write the children's names on the bags to identify them later.

HomeLink: Genesis 28:10-22

Jacob slept with his head on a rock and dreamed of an angelic stairway. God showed His love to Jacob by making a wonderful promise: "I will be with you wherever you go." The stone reminder can help your child remember that God loves him or her too!

Play the following game with your child. Use a folded blanket for a stone pillow. **Pretend to be Jacob traveling. Now be Jacob sleeping, using a stone for a pillow. Show me the angels going up and down the staircase. God said, "I am the Lord. I will be with you wherever you go." Show me Jacob praying to God.**

BCE43: Noah and the Flood Mural, Part 1

Supplies: Copies of the HomeLink · Butcher paper · Masking tape · Overhead projector · Permanent marker · Washable markers or paints (your choice) · Pictures of animals that can be cut out (from magazines, coloring books, etc.) · Scissors · Glue

Preparation: Tape a long length of butcher paper to a wall. Use an overhead projector to enlarge the ark picture below by projecting it on the paper and tracing it with a permanent marker.

Directions: The children will complete this mural over the course of two weeks. Show the children the ark outline on the butcher paper, and explain that they will be adding color as well as animals around the ark and any other details they like. After next week's Bible story, the children will add a rainbow.

Let children choose which part of the mural they wish to work on this week. Some may draw on background details (sky, land), some may color (or paint), and others may cut out animal pictures to glue on or even draw their own animals to glue on. Put Park Patrol helpers in charge of each segment of the work.

Be sure each child takes a HomeLink paragraph home today.

HomeLink: Genesis 6:5–22; 7:11–17, 24

Noah loved and obeyed God, even when he was the only one left! And God kept Noah safe. Before God sent a huge flood to cover all the earth, He helped Noah build an ark for himself, his family, and certain animals.

God loves you too and cares about your safety. Pray with your parents to thank God for all the ways He loves and protects you. Be sure to tell your parents about the mural, and invite them to come and see it!

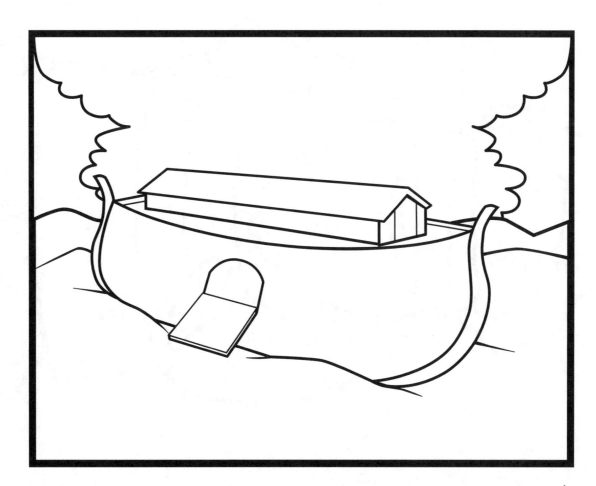

BCP43: Noah Hand Puppet

Supplies: Copies of the Noah puppet and HomeLink · Lunch-size paper bags · Crayons · Glue · Optional: cotton balls or batting

Preparation: Make a copy of the puppet pieces and a HomeLink for each child. Cut out the puppet pieces.

Directions: Give each child one set of puppet pieces to color. Show the children how to glue the puppet pieces to the bag. Children may glue cotton balls or batting to the puppet's hair and beard. The HomeLink should be glued to the back of the puppet. Help the children make their puppets "talk" by moving the flap of the bag with their fingers.

HomeLink: Genesis 6:5-22; 7:11-17, 24

Encourage your child to use the Noah puppet, as well as blocks and plastic animals, to act out the Bible story.

God told Noah to build an ark. (Let your child put the puppet on one hand and build with the other hand.) **Noah put food on the ark. God sent animals for Noah to put on the ark. Noah and his family moved there too. Then God shut the door.**

It rained until water covered the earth. God kept Noah, his family, and the animals safe on the ark. God loved Noah. God loves us.

BCE44: Noah and the Flood Mural, Part 2

Supplies: The mural started last week · Tissue paper in rainbow colors · Glue · Washable markers or paints · Copies of the HomeLink Invitations · Optional: animal pictures that can be cut out, gray construction paper or paper stones from Bible story

Preparation: If necessary, tape up the mural again in a place where the children can work on it. Make copies of the HomeLink paragraph.

Directions: This is the second week for the children to work on the mural. This week they will add a rainbow and may add more details as time permits.

Let all the children have a hand in adding part of the rainbow to the mural, by gluing on small pieces of colorful tissue paper. Make the rainbow huge, stretching all the way across the top of the mural. You may want to draw the outline to show where the colors go, or simply let the children add colors in a rainbow shape.

You might also choose to let the children add a stone altar, cut from construction paper or using the stones from the Elementary Bible Story. As time permits, children may add more animals milling around the ark. The children may wish to also sign their names to the mural.

Be sure to send HomeLink invitations home with the children after letting them fill out the location of the mural within your church.

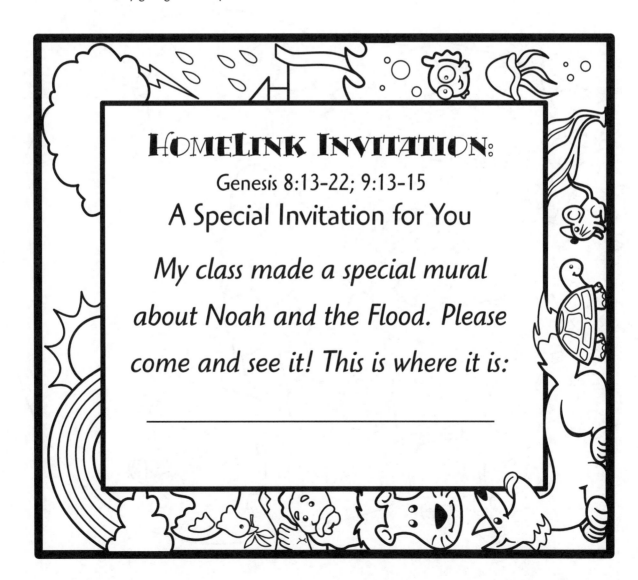

HomeLink Invitation:

Genesis 8:13-22; 9:13-15

A Special Invitation for You

My class made a special mural about Noah and the Flood. Please come and see it! This is where it is:

_____

BCP44: Rainbow Banner

Supplies: Copies of the picture below and HomeLink · 8" paper plates · Crayons · Glue · Crepe paper streamers in rainbow colors · Stapler

Preparation: Cut out a picture and a HomeLink for each child. Cut the streamers to lengths of 14". Each banner will need four different colors of streamers.

Directions: Give each child a picture to color. Help the children glue their pictures to the middle of a plate. Help each child staple four streamers to the bottom of the plate. Ask the children to glue their HomeLinks to the backs of the plates.

HomeLink: Genesis 8:13-22; 9:13-15

Let your child use the Rainbow Banner to help him or her remember the following story.

Noah and his family and the animals were on the ark. It rained for 40 days and 40 nights. Water covered everything. After it stopped raining, the water went away. Then Noah, his family, and all the animals left the ark. Noah built an altar to worship. Noah and his family thanked God. God put a rainbow in the sky. We can thank God to show our love for Him.

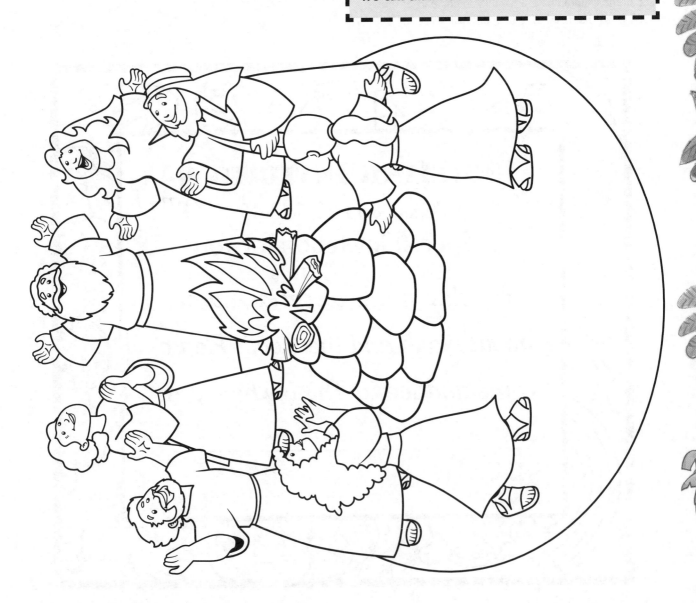

BCE45: My Favorite Bible Verses

Supplies: Copy of the book covers for each child · Colored markers or pencils · Plain white paper · Scissors · Hole punch · Yarn · Bibles · Optional: concordance

Preparation: Make a copy of the book covers below for each child. Cut plain white paper into rectangles approximately 3" x 4". Cut enough of the white paper so that each child can have at least five pieces. These will be the pages of their books. Cut yarn into 6" pieces, two for each child. Make a sample booklet for the children to follow. Be prepared to suggest "favorite" Bible verses to the children.

Directions: Talk with the children about their favorite Bible verses. Older children may be able to quote references or say some from memory. You will have to help younger children find their favorite verses based on

the phrases they remember. Feel free to offer suggestions of verses that children tend to like, such as Psalm 23:1; Psalm 145:8; Matthew 28:20; John 3:16; 1 John 3:1. They should write out a few favorite verses and leave some sheets blank for future use. Be aware that early elementary children write very slowly; offer help as necessary, but let them enjoy doing their own work.

Give each child a copy of the front and back covers to color and cut out. (The HomeLink is printed on the back cover.) Help the children stack their papers between the two covers, making sure the edges are even. Help the children punch two holes on the left edge as indicated on the front cover. Then tie a short piece of yarn through each hole. The children may write their names on the back cover.

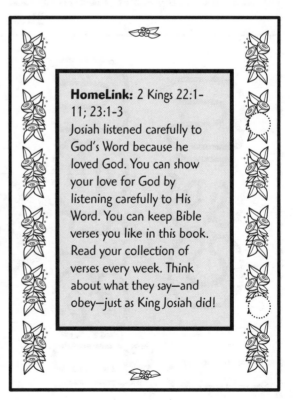

HomeLink: 2 Kings 22:1-11; 23:1-3
Josiah listened carefully to God's Word because he loved God. You can show your love for God by listening carefully to His Word. You can keep Bible verses you like in this book. Read your collection of verses every week. Think about what they say—and obey—just as King Josiah did!

BCP45: Bible Scroll

Supplies: Copy of the scroll and HomeLink for each child · Washable markers · Two unsharpened pencils or dowel rods for each child · Tape · Two pieces of 6" x 11" paper for each child · Yarn · Glue sticks

Preparation: Copy and cut out the scroll and HomeLink for each child. Tape a piece of paper to each short end of a scroll. This will create a long piece for each child. Cut a 10" piece of yarn or string for each child.

Directions: Give each child a scroll paper to color. Let the children glue the HomeLinks to the backs of their papers. Then help the children tape a pencil or dowel rod to each end. Show the children how to roll up the scroll around each pencil until the rolls meet in the middle. Tie the scroll together with a piece of yarn.

HomeLink: 2 Kings 22:1-11; 23:1-3

Josiah found the Book of the Law and read it to the people. Reading God's Word is one way we show our love to God. Help your child review the Bible story throughout the week.

Josiah was the king. He fixed up the temple where God's people worshiped. One of the workers found a scroll. It was God's Word! King Josiah and the people listened to God's Word. We can listen to God's Word too. Let your child pretend to be King Josiah reading to the people.

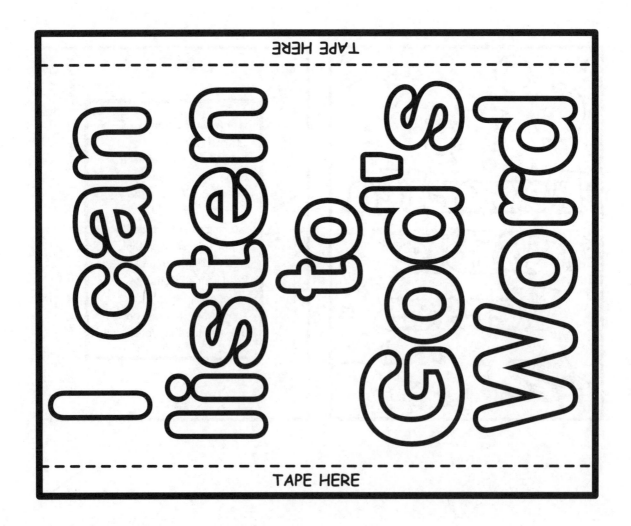

TAPE HERE

TAPE HERE

BCE46: Sea Scene

Supplies: Copies of the sea scene below · Scissors · Markers or crayons · Construction paper · Glue · Blue cellophane

Preparation: Make a copy of the sea scene for each child. Cut blue cellophane about an inch wider and just as tall as the sea scene, one for each child

Directions: Let each child color a copy of the sea scene.

Have the children glue their sea scenes centered on a piece of construction paper. Help the children each glue a piece of blue cellophane over their sea scene. Talk about how covering the picture in blue changes the colors underneath. Read together the title and HomeLink, and talk about ways the children can obey God.

Jonah Learned to Obey God

HomeLink: Jonah 1–3   Obeying God shows that we love Him. How can you obey God this week? Talk it over with your parents as you show them your artwork.

BCP46: Jonah Windsock

Supplies: Copies of the fish and HomeLink · Crayons · Crepe paper streamers · Stapler · Hole punch · Yarn

Preparation: Copy the fish and HomeLinks for each child. Cut two crepe paper streamers, each 12" long, for each child. Cut a 10-inch-long piece of yarn for each child.

Directions: Give each child a fish to color. When done, help the children staple two pieces of streamer to the tails of the fish. Punch a hole near the fishes' mouths. Tie a piece of yarn through each hole. Glue a HomeLink to the back of each child's fish.

HomeLink: Jonah 1—3 Jonah learned to obey God. Hang the windsock in a prominent place to reinforce the lesson for your child. Review the following story throughout the week.

God told Jonah to go tell the people of Nineveh to obey the Lord. But Jonah took a boat going the other way. God sent a storm. Jonah had the sailors throw him out of the boat. The storm stopped. God sent a big fish to swallow Jonah. Jonah thanked God for saving him. God made the fish cough Jonah onto a beach. Then Jonah gave God's message to Nineveh. Jonah showed his love for God when he obeyed God. Obeying shows we love God.

BCE47: Yes/No Puppets

Supplies: Copies of the puppet figures and HomeLinks · Colored markers or crayons · Scissors · Craft sticks · Glue · Optional: yarn in hair colors, fabric scraps

Preparation: Make a copy of both puppet figures below and a HomeLink for each child.

Directions: Give each child a "yes" and a "no" puppet to color. Encourage the children to color the puppet to resemble themselves. If you'd like, let the children glue on yarn for hair and fabric scraps for clothes.

When finished decorating their puppets, the children cut them out and glue them back-to-back on a craft stick, leaving a handle sticking out at the bottom.

Ask the children to name choices they face each week. Using their puppets, the children can express their feelings and the choices they would make. Be sure all the kids take a HomeLink home with their puppets.

HomeLink: 1 Kings 3:1-15

Yes! No! What's a good choice? You have to make choices every day. The best way to make a good choice is to talk it over with God.

This week, look for a choice each day. Talk through it with your parents. Then pray together about it. Ask God to help you make wise choices.

BCP47: King Solomon's Crown

Supplies: Copies of the crown pattern and HomeLink · Heavy cardstock or craft foam · 1-inch wide elastic · Craft glue · Large sequins or scraps of craft foam · Stapler · Small containers · Cotton swabs

Preparation: Make a copy of the HomeLink for each child. Make one copy of the crown to use as a pattern on either heavy cardstock or craft foam. For each child in your class, trace around the pattern and cut out the crown. Put a small amount of craft glue in each container.

Directions: Give each child a crown to decorate with sequins and foam scraps. Put a small amount of glue in each container, and show the children how to dip a cotton swab in the glue, then dab the glue onto what they are attaching. Measure elastic to fit the back of each

child's head. Staple the elastic to the ends of the crown. Glue a HomeLink to the back of each crown.

HomeLink: 1 Kings 3:1-15

Solomon was the wisest king ever! Let your child pretend to be King Solomon, wearing the crown, while acting out the following story:

You are King Solomon. One night you are sleeping. God tells you that He will give you whatever you ask. What do you want? *(Wisdom.)* **God is pleased with what you asked for. He will make you wise. He will help you make good choices.**

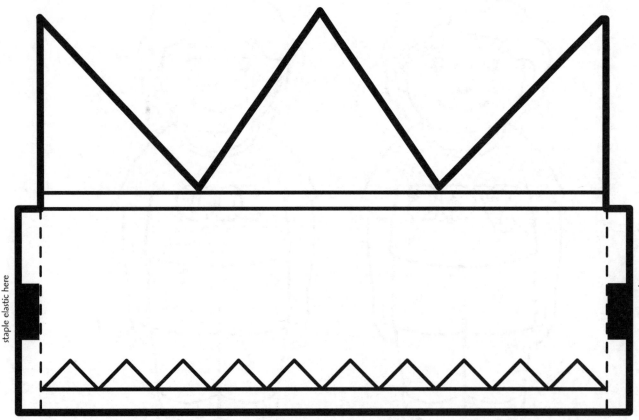

staple elastic here

staple elastic here

BCE48: Psalm 23 Rebus

Supplies: Copy of your Psalm 23 rebus, the pictures below, and HomeLink for each child · Markers or crayons · Scissors · Glue

Preparation: To make the rebus, type or print Psalm 23 from the Bible translation of your choice. Use large letters and spread out the words, making it fill an 8 1/2" x 11" page. Leave out the following seven words, allowing space for a picture to be glued on: *shepherd, paths, water, staff, table, days, house.* Make enough copies of the Psalm 23 rebus for all the children. Also make copies of the patterns provided below and HomeLink for each child.

Directions: Give each child a copy of the Psalm 23 rebus and read it together. Then give each child a copy of the seven pictures. Let the kids color the pictures and cut them out. Help the children find the right spots in the rebus to glue their pictures. Have the children glue the HomeLink on the bottom or back of the page.

> **HomeLink:** Psalm 23
>
> This week, be like David! Find a creative way to tell the Lord that you love Him and trust His care for you. David sang songs to God. What could you do? Talk it over with your parents. Try a new idea!

BCP48: Shepherd Stained-Glass Picture

Supplies: Copy of the shepherd picture and a HomeLink for each child · Colored pencils · Cotton balls · Vegetable oil · Waxed paper

Preparation: Make a sample craft so you know how it will work in class.

Directions: Set a piece of waxed paper in front of each child to use as a placemat. Lay a shepherd picture on top of each "placemat." Let the children color their pictures with colored pencils. When done, help each child use a cotton ball to dab a small amount of vegetable oil over the surface of the picture. This will give it a translucent look. Send the pictures home on the waxed paper along with a copy of the HomeLink.

HomeLink: Psalm 23

We can trust God to care for us, as a shepherd cares for his sheep. You may want to display the stained glass picture in a window. Tell your child this simple version of the psalm throughout the week.

The Lord is my shepherd. He gives me everything I need. He gives me food to eat. He gives me water to drink. He helps me rest when I'm tired. I will not be afraid. God takes care of me wherever I go. He will love me all of my life. I will live with Him forever.

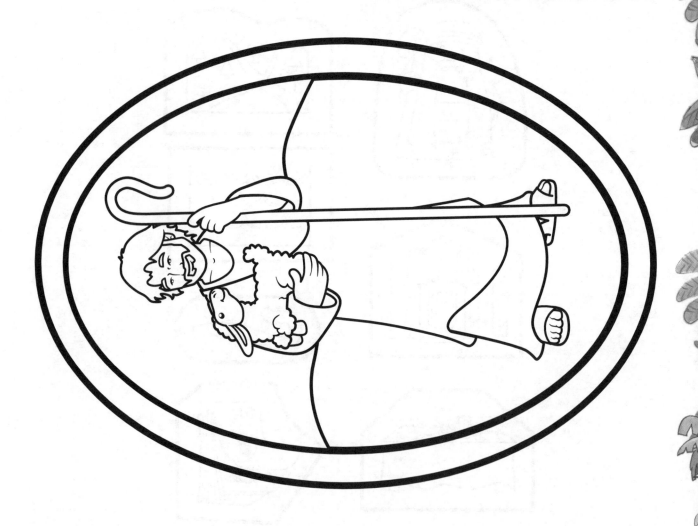

BCE49: Windsock

Supplies: Copies of the windsock band and HomeLink · Construction paper · Scissors · Colored markers · Glue · Stapler · Colorful crepe paper · Hole punch · String or yarn

Preparation: Make a copy of the windsock band, small figures, and HomeLink for each child. Cut construction paper or craft foam into strips about 12" x 4". Cut crepe paper streamers about 12" long, 4 - 6 per child.

Directions: Give each child a windsock band and small figures to color. When finished, have the children glue their band onto the top third of the construction paper or craft foam strip. Next, have them glue the HomeLink to the bottom third of the construction paper. Then, have them glue the figures in various places to decorate the band. Show the children how to bend their strip into a circle and staple or glue the ends together.

Let the children choose crepe paper streamers to glue onto the bottom of their windsock band. At three equal points at the top of the windsock band, punch a hole. Tie a length of string or yarn in each; then tie the three loose ends together in a knot.

Encourage the children to hang their windsock at home where it will remind them to love God and others.

HomeLink: Mark 12:28-34
Jesus taught that we should love God and each other. We should love God with all that we are—our heart, soul, mind, and strength. We should love and care for others as we love ourselves. Talk to your parents this week about how you can love God and others better.

I'll Love God With All My Heart, Soul, Mind, And Strength.

BCP49: Jesus and Teacher Finger Puppets

Supplies: Copies of the puppets and HomeLink · Crayons · Clear tape · Resealable plastic bags

Preparation: Copy and cut out two finger puppets and a HomeLink for each child.

Directions: Give each child a set of finger puppets. Show the kids how to color both sides of a puppet the same. Help the children fit their puppets over a finger and tape the top and sides. Let each child bring home a set of puppets and a HomeLink in a resealable plastic bag.

HomeLink: Mark 12:28-34

Jesus taught that we are to love God and each other. Help your child review the Bible story during the week using the finger puppets.

Jesus went to the temple. Put on the Jesus finger puppet. **A teacher asked Him what the most important rule was.** Put on the teacher finger puppet. **Jesus told the man to love God will all his heart, soul, mind, and strength. Jesus also told the man to love others as much as he loves himself. We also are to love God and each other.**

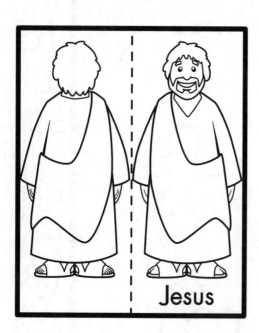

Jesus

Teacher

BCE50: Forgiving Friend Bag Puppets

Supplies: Copies of the puppet pieces and HomeLink · Lunch-size paper bags · Scissors · Glue · Crayons or markers · Yarn · Fabric scraps · Copies of Teacher Feature skits

Preparation: Make a copy of the puppet pieces and a HomeLink for each child. Make additional copies of the skits from Teacher Feature on index cards or paper.

Directions: Give each child a set of puppet pieces to cut out. Show the kids how to glue the pieces to a paper bag. They may color the pieces and add yarn for hair and fabric scraps for clothing. Encourage the kids to make the pieces look like themselves. Have each child glue a HomeLink to the back of their puppet.

When completed, give out copies of the skits. The children should use their puppets to practice saying, "I forgive you," when put in any of the scenarios described on the skits. The children may make up their own appropriate forgiveness skits as well. Let each child take home a skit.

HomeLink: Matthew 18:21-35

Love means we keep on forgiving. Sometimes it's hard, but it's important. This week, read the Bible story with a parent. Use your puppet to help you practice a time when you need to forgive. Pray together about forgiving others.

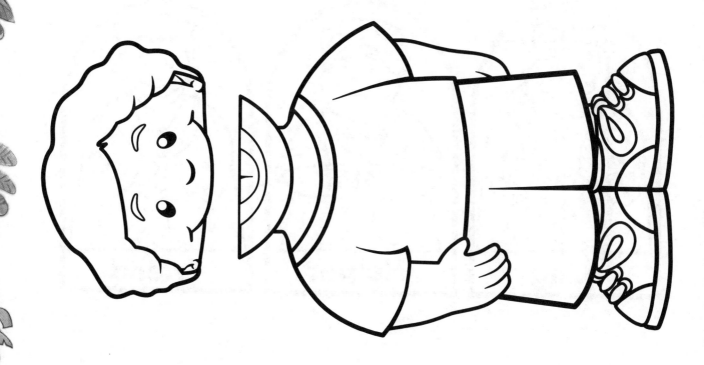

BCP50: Forgiving Hand Puppets

Supplies: Copies of the puppets and HomeLink · Scissors · Colored pencils · Resealable plastic bag · Optional: cardstock

Preparation: Make a copy of the three puppets for each child. You may want to use cardstock for sturdier puppets. Cut out all the puppets, including the finger holes. Also copy the HomeLink for each child.

Directions: Give each child a set of three puppets. As the children color their puppets, review the Bible story with the children by asking questions about each puppet. Have each child put their puppets and a HomeLink in a resealable plastic bag to take home.

HomeLink: Matthew 18:21-34

Love means we keep on forgiving. Jesus taught that we should forgive others over and over. Let your child wear the hand puppets to act out the Bible story:

Jesus used a story to teach Peter that love means we keep on forgiving. Once there was a king. His helper had borrowed a lot of money from him. The helper couldn't pay it back, so the king forgave him all the money he owed. The helper had a friend. The friend borrowed a couple of dollars from the helper. When the friend couldn't pay him back, the helper wouldn't forgive his friend. The king had the bad helper put into jail.

King

Helper

Friend

BCE51: Gift Basket Service Project

Supplies: Basket (or box) · Items for a needy family · Tissue paper · Stamps and inkpads · Stickers · Ribbon · Optional: greeting card

Preparation: Plan to give a gift basket to a needy family in your church, or plan on a few smaller baskets that can be given to church shut-ins. Consider giving to the same people that your class prayed for during Share and Prayer. If possible, send a note to your students' homes during the week before class asking them to donate specific items for the basket. Make arrangements to deliver the completed basket(s).

Directions: Tell the children about this service project: They will be decorating a basket to give to a needy family or individuals. If you haven't already done so, briefly tell the children about the family or individuals. Set out the basket and the items, and let the kids tell why those items would be good in the basket. Then let the children fill the basket. As an option, use the tissue paper inside the basket and fill the basket after the next step is completed.

Spread out sheets of tissue paper on the table, and let the children decorate it by stamping decorative pictures on it. They may also add stickers. When finished, help the children set the basket on the paper, draw the loose ends toward the top, and secure it with ribbon. As an option, put the tissue paper into the basket and fill it. Put the ribbon on a handle to decorate if you wish. You may wish to have the children sign a card saying who the gift is from.

Be sure to give each child a HomeLink to take home.

HomeLink: 1 Corinthians 16:1-3; 2 Corinthians 8:1-7; 9:7-12

God wants us to give cheerfully to those in need. This week you gave up doing your own craft so you could give a beautiful gift to a needy person. You can keep on giving by praying for that person during the week.

This week, read the Bible story again with your parents. Talk about how you feel when you give to God's work and other times that you can give.

BCP51: Offering Bank

Supplies: Copies of the label and HomeLink · An empty 12-oz. juice can for each child · Crayons · Glue

Preparation: Copy the label and HomeLink for each child, and cut them out. Wash and dry the juice cans.

Directions: The people in our Bible story showed love to one another by giving money to help poor Christians. We can show love to others by putting money in a special offering bank to give to people who need it. Give each child a label to color. Show the children how to put glue on a can and then smooth a label (with the HomeLink still attached) over it. Talk about how the children can use this offering bank at home: Their whole family can add coins to it and choose who to give it to.

HomeLink: 1 Corinthians 16:1-3; 2 Corinthians 8:1-7; 9:7-12

The Christians in Corinth and other towns gave money to help poor Christians in Jerusalem. Use this offering bank as a family to collect money, and together choose an organization or a needy family to donate the money to. Review the Bible story with your child during the week.

The Christians in Jerusalem needed food and money. Paul told other churches about the people in Jerusalem. Even though some of the people didn't have much money, they gave what they could. The people in Corinth happily gave money too. Paul and some men from Corinth brought the money to Jerusalem. The people in Jerusalem were happy that other people showed love to them. We can give cheerfully to those in need.

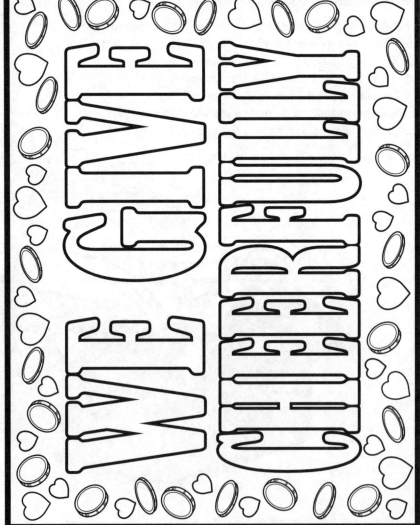

BCE52: Paul and Lydia Action Figures

Supplies: Copies of the action figures, accessories, and HomeLink · Scissors · Fabric scraps · Glue · Resealable plastic bags · Optional: colored markers

Preparation: Copy the Paul and Lydia figures on stiff paper for each child. If your time is short or if you use cardboard, you may want to cut them out ahead of time. Also make copies of the HomeLink.

Directions: Give each child a set of Paul and Lydia figures and accessories to cut out. Let the children choose fabric scraps and cut them to fit the clothing and accessories. The children glue the scraps to their pieces. As an option, you may have the children simply color the figures.

Show the children how to fold the side tabs to make Paul and Lydia stand. Let the children use their figures to retell the Bible story. Send each child's action figures home in a resealable plastic bag to keep the pieces together, along with a HomeLink.

HomeLink: Acts 16:10-15

Sharing what we have shows love. And God wants us to learn to love one another. This week, read the Bible story with your parents. Use your action figures to act it out for them.

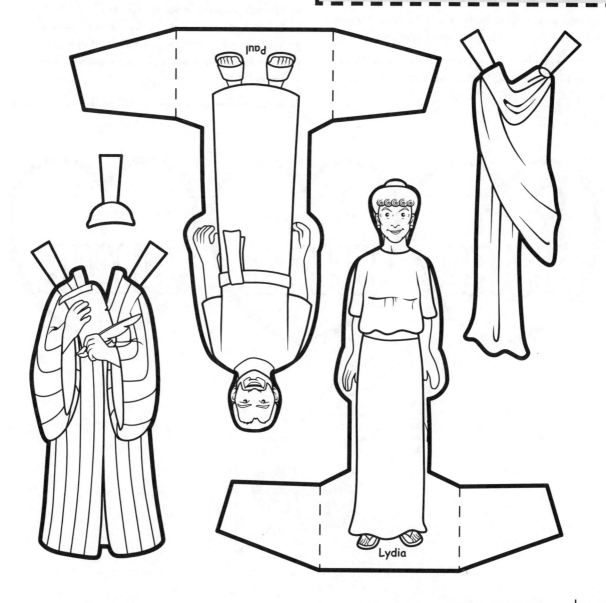

BCP52: Sharing Reminder Bracelets

Supplies: White cardstock or purple craft foam · Hole punch or sharp scissors · 1/8" elastic or elastic cord · Crayons · Purple pony beads · Copies of the HomeLink

Preparation: Copy the three hearts below onto cardstock or craft foam for each child. Cut out the hearts. Punch a small hole in each heart at the small circle. Cut lengths of elastic eight inches long. Also copy a HomeLink for each child.

Directions: Give each child a set of hearts. If using cardstock, let the children color them. Give each child a length of elastic, and help the children thread it through the hearts, with a pony bead between each heart. As the children work, remind them that Lydia from the Bible story sold purple cloth. Tie the elastic to make a bracelet, making sure there is enough room to take it off.

Talk to the children about wearing the bracelet during the week as a reminder to share with others. Send a HomeLink home with each child.

HomeLink: Acts 16:10-15

Sharing what we have shows love. Paul shared with Lydia about Jesus. Lydia shared her home with Paul and his friends.

Let your child wear the bracelet made in class as a reminder to share. Act out the following story to review the Bible story with your child during the week. You can use cloths or scarves to represent Bible-time clothes.

Paul and his friends were looking for a place to pray by the river. They saw Lydia and her friends praying. Paul shared with them about Jesus. Lydia and her family were baptized. Lydia shared her home with Paul and his friends. Sharing what we have shows God's love.

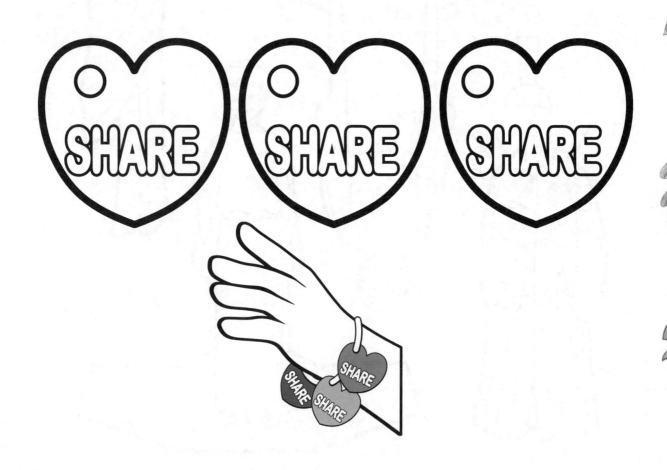